DHARMA IN HELL

THE PRISON WRITINGS OF FLEET MAULL

by *Fleet Maull*

KATE CRISP, EDITOR

PRISON DHARMA NEWORK
Boulder
2005

PRISON DHARMA NETWORK
PO Box 4623
Boulder, CO 80306
www.PrisonDharmaNetwork.org

ISBN: 0-9718143-1-7

First Published November 2005

Distributed by Prison Dharma Network.

Cover Design by Mary Sweet

Printed in the United States of America

DEDICATION

This book is dedicated to my root teacher, Chogyam Trungpa
Rinpoche, and to all the prisoners and staff who daily face the
challenge of surviving in the hell realms of our prisons and
jails, where the spirit—to say nothing of the mind and body—
suffers the continual assault of dehumanization and violence.

It is especially dedicated to those prisoners and staff who
courageously practice kindness and compassion in the face of
this relentless assault on the human spirit.

Dharma in Hell

ACKNOWLEDGEMENTS

This book would not have been possible without the tireless efforts and unflagging inspiration of my editor, Kate Crisp. Kate conceived of this project and skillfully shepherded it from beginning to end with her keen sense of what is most important and relevant to the spiritual quest and struggles of prisoners, a sensibility honed through her many years of dedicated service to prisoners as director of Prison Dharma Network. The book would also not have been possible without the kindness of a number of editors and publishers who gave me the opportunity to write for their publications while in prison: Melvin McLeod and Molly DeShong of the *Shambhala Sun*, Susan Moon of *Turning Wheel*, and Rabbi Michael Lerner of *Tikkun Magazine*. I was particularly inspired in my writing by my friend and mentor, Bo Lozoff, who has kindly written the foreword for *Dharma in Hell*, and whose book, *We're All Doing Time*, was a faithful companion and continual inspiration during my time behind the walls. I am deeply indebted to my two very dear friends, Karen Lavin and Dan Barrett, for the continual and unwavering kindness and support they provided throughout my prison journey, always encouraging me in my writing and projects. I am particularly grateful to Dan Barrett for serving as the volunteer coordinator for Prison Dharma Network from 1991 to 1999.

My prison writings were inspired by my spiritual practice, my service work, and the "rock meets bone" realities of long-term incarceration. I am deeply indebted to my spiritual teachers and friends who so kindly supported my journey. The late Vajra Regent Osel Tendzin, visited me in prison in 1987, giving me the necessary empowerments to continue and complete my ngondro (*preliminary*) practices on the Tibetan Buddhist vajrayana path. Practicing like "my hair was on fire," I completed those practices in 1988, driven by the devastation and longing I experienced following the death of my guru, Chogyam Trungpa Rinpoche. All that I was able to accomplish in prison and since, is nothing more than my very limited and imperfect expression of the profound teachings, example, and blessings of my teacher. Then, in 1989 the Venerable Thrangu Rinpoche kindly visited the prison to perform the Vajrayogini Abhisheka (*empowerment*) for me, so that I could begin deity yoga sadhana practice, the next stage on the vajrayana path. This practice, more than anything else, shifted my prison experience into a profound path of transformation. I can't begin to express my gratitude to Thrangu Rinpoche for his great kindness.

Inspired by his unique integration of spirituality and social action, I contacted Roshi Bernie Glassman, co-founder along with his late wife Roshi Sandra Jishu Holmes of the Zen Peacemaker Order, asking him to join this new order. I wasn't looking for another spiritual path, as I was certainly in no need of more practices or further inspiration beyond the depth and richness of the Tibetan Buddhist tradition I had so fortunately encountered. I was simply taken with the possibility of a fully ordained path of service in the streets. With the permission of my Tibetan Buddhist teachers, I began studying with Roshi Glassman and

Sensei Holmes in 1994. They visited me in prison several times per year and corresponded with me regularly, guiding my Zen training, practice and study, and affirming my dedication to service and peacemaking while in prison. I received the Jukai vows in 1995 and was ordained a Zen Peacemaker Priest in 1997 in a ceremony presided over by Roshi Glassman and Sensei Jishu in the prison chapel. I am deeply grateful to Jishu who showed me so much kindness, and I continue to study with Roshi Glassman, or "Bernie" as he prefers to be called.

I would also like to express my gratitude to the many spiritual friends and fellow practitioners who visited me in prison and/or corresponded with me while I was there, offering their support and friendship, including, to name but a few: Pema Chodron, Stephen & Ondrea Levine, Elizabeth Kubler-Ross, Bill Bothwell, Purna Steinitz, Peter Volz, Sister Dipa, James & Carolyn Gimian, Mitchell Levy, Liz Craig, Nancy Craig, Pamela Krasney, John & Lisa Bayless, Michael O'Keefe, Dave Gold, David Rome, Judith Simmer-Brown, and Marianna Kaplan.

Finally, I would like to acknowledge my family who stuck with me through it all, and especially my son, Robert Maull, who despite the obvious challenge of growing up with his father in prison, has become an amazing young man, a good son and a continual inspiration to a grateful father.

Fleet Maull
Boulder, Colorado
August 2005

Dharma in Hell

CONTENTS

FORWARD
By Bo Lozoff

The Greek legend of Sisyphus has always intrigued me. For various reasons the Gods sentence Sisyphus to an eternity of rolling a huge boulder up a mountain with his bare shoulders, reaching the top, and watching the boulder roll all the way down again. Sisyphus then dutifully trudges back down to do it again. And again. And again....

Those of us who live or work in prisons, or who are committed to helping those who do, may often feel like a modern-day Sisyphus. For all our devotion, for all our efforts to change and humanize the system, the prison system doesn't get better, it just rolls back down to the bottom and, in fact, gets worse. And just when you think it can't get much worse, along comes a Sheriff Joe Arpaio who dresses inmates up in pink and humiliates them in every way he can; or along come the business moguls who dreamed up the monstrous idea of the private prison industry. It seems the bottom keeps getting lower and the top keeps extending

11

farther out of sight. But we continue to roll that boulder none the less.

In 1973, when I began working in prisons, there were about 185,000 prison inmates in adult institutions across the United States. Now, California has nearly that many. Texas has nearly that many. The U.S. grand total tops two *million* people who are locked behind bars. College students frequently ask me the reason for this disgraceful state of affairs, and my answer is usually, "Because we're just really stupid. Unbelievably stupid." Prisons harm people and long sentences incapacitate people. And so we build more and more prisons and sentence inmates to longer and longer terms. And then we release over 90% of those damaged, incapacitated people with little more than a few dollars in "gate money" and the clothes on their backs. If that's not stupid, what is?

But back to Sisyphus. No one has forced me or my wife to work in such a stupid milieu for over thirty years. We could easily have done our bit for five or ten years and gone on to a more positive field of endeavor, one where we might actually be able to improve something—literacy, vocational training, working with kids—who knows? So, why have we continued to roll this boulder up such a depressing mountain for all these years?

The answer is simple: Because for some mysterious reason of human nature, the very horror of such a bleak and maddening prison system seems to inspire and fuel a level of spiritual growth, sometimes even total transformation, that is unparalleled in any other context. An opening remark to the many thousands of prisoners in my workshops has been "Here's the deal: Life is very deep, and you haven't been acting like it. Let's talk about that." And we do. We talk like oldest and best friends. We have magical conversations of the sort that are always taking place somewhere in the world, usually in a hidden cave or a remote *ashram* or under an ancient tree or on top of a mountain or in a quiet little sanctuary. Without a doubt, the most wonderful, sincere, *honest* conversations of my life have been inside terrible prisons, with human beings who have never before taken the time to consider any philosophical view or spiritual dimension whatsoever. Interestingly enough, the worse the prison, the more magical the conversations. People in Hell have no energy to waste on pleasantries or beating around the bush. They desperately need to know whether *anything* truly good, genuinely comforting, exists. They need to rip off all the wrapping and see whether there is indeed a gift inside the box.

Fortunately, the gift is real and it is there, and it is more powerful than anything they had ever expected. I have heard comments, or received letters, from *tens of thousands* of prisoners, each assuming it was the first time anyone had ever said this: "I know it sounds crazy, but I am happier and feel more free right here in lockup than I have ever felt in my life." Imagine that. Many of those people do get out eventually, and many do not. The ones who do often seek work in the helping professions, especially in recovery or working with at-risk youth. The ones who will never get out of prison become genuine elders in their prison communities, peacekeepers and counselors to the legions of confused and frightened people who surround them.

This is the magic of spiritual work in prison, or as Fleet Maull puts it, *Dharma in Hell*, that keeps all of us Sisyphus wanna-be's rolling those boulders up the mountain. We and our prison friends find the Holy together. We touch the Sacred. We share the profound goodwill that makes Jesus beam from ear to ear. We unlock insights and levels of perception that have the Buddha smiling down on us.

Anywhere that such experiences happen is not Hell, but Heaven. It may be Hell again a moment later, and it may be designed and constructed from the beginning to be Hell, but we can turn it into Heaven in an instant. And some of the prison elders I am privileged to know, have found the strength and clarity to keep it as Heaven day after day after day as they make peace with their prison existence—and their opportunity for service there—as what the Hindus call one's "Karma Bhoomi," or "destined field of action."

Fleet Maull saw the opportunity to turn Hell into Heaven for himself and many dying prisoners, and he went for it. And so the prison hospice movement was born. A friend of mine, whom Fleet has probably never met or heard of, spent over thirty years in Oregon's state prisons, and it was hospice work that finally brought dignity and great meaning to his existence there. It is a certainty that Fleet's hospice work in the federal system helped bring about that opportunity. Similarly, I constantly hear from or meet people who tell me some profound transformation in their lives that came about as a result of the Prison-Ashram Project, and I'd never have had any way of knowing about it if I hadn't run into them quite by chance. Heaven works like that. Good works spin and spin in intersecting circles forever, even when it sometimes may appear that we're pushing one single boulder up an ungrateful mountain where it falls back down again.

Bo Lozoff is the director of the Prison-Ashram Project and the Human Kindness Foundation. He is the author of We're All Doing Time. *See www.HumanKindness.org for more information.*

INTRODUCTION
by Michael O'Keefe

Among American Buddhist practitioners there is a common lament concerning the volume of practices that must be completed in order to realize the promise of Buddhism. In the face of balancing all these practices with our everyday lives, an idea comes up that has a perverse appeal. "If I ever get sentenced to prison, I might have a chance—otherwise I'm just gonna bide my time. Maybe in my next lifetime I'll gain enlightenment. Until then, why worry?"

For Fleet Maull that idea became a reality. In 1985 he was given thirty years for drug smuggling. Fleet was sentenced under a statute that convicts the 'Kingpin' of a drug smuggling enterprise. He doesn't deny his life as a drug smuggler, but contends that an overzealous D.A.'s office—that spent close to $500,000 putting together a case against him—used the new statutes to set him up as a living example of the 'Just Say No!' philosophy of the Reagan Administration. 'If you can't say no—say good-bye' was the message. Fleet doesn't deny dealing drugs, but is adamant he was *not* a kingpin. He knew of his impending arrest and had ample time to split the U.S. permanently and continue life as an expatriate, but he chose to face his arrest, trial, and sentencing not as a smuggler might—but as a Buddhist facing his karma.

When Fleet began his sentence in 1985, he had already studied extensively with Chogyam Trungpa Rinpoche and been a practicing Buddhist since 1978. It may seem incongruous that a Buddhist practitioner could be involved in cocaine trafficking, but we should understand the context of someone's life before we judge it.

Like a lot of us at that time, Fleet's ideals were formed during the 1960's when the counterculture offered disaffected youth a way of finding itself. At that time the U.S. was a country that saw nothing unethical or immoral about conducting a war with dubious motives, or allowing centuries of bigotry and hatred to continue. The counterculture of the sixties formed as a way of 'Just Saying No!' to all of that. And saying 'Yes!' to: compassion, human rights, and equality for all people and nations.

One ritual of acceptance into the counterculture was drug use, and although we now know the insidious nature of addiction and the tragedy it creates, back then, getting high was a way of connecting to a larger sense of self that we hoped would facilitate a transition from hypocritical Americans, to real patriots. As naïve and misdirected as that may sound, it was a pervasive sentiment at the time.

In retrospect, the trap a lot of us missed made us members of an endangered species. Payment would be extracted with membership dues that came at a steep price. For some, it was simply good times, but others risked and lost their sanity and even their lives from drug use. Still others found a way to walk between the cracks and survive. Fleet fell into the latter category but not without serious consequences.

During his incarceration Fleet faced many demons, not the least of which was his own drug addiction and alcoholism, which is one of the many things he turned around in prison. One of the most notable transformations of Fleet Maull was fueled by his aspiration to be of service to other prisoners in need. Fleet was a hospice worker while in prison and founded the National Prison Hospice Association. If there is a good place to die, prison isn't it. Fleet had a vision to create a safe, sane, and caring environment for dying prisoners and brought it to fruition.

He also founded the Prison Dharma Network (PDN) in 1987, an organization that is flourishing today and whose spiritual advisory board reads like a Who's Who of worldwide spirituality—Robert Aitken Roshi, Thrangu Rinpoche, Roshi Bernie Glassman, Father Thomas Keating, Jon Kabat Zinn, Rabbi David Cooper, and Pema Chodron—are just a few of the dharma heavyweights involved. PDN's mission is to provide support for prisoners seeking a contemplative path.

Fleet was released in 1999 and is currently the Director of the Peacemaker Community Colorado, he teaches at Naropa University, and is nearing completion of his Ph.D. in Psychology. He also travels extensively as a prison activist and speaker.

Fleet was transformed from a part-time Buddhist and drug smuggler to a full-time Buddhist teacher and leader who's path is to create peace and freedom behind bars.

A Zen master was once asked by a student, "Where do you go when you die?"
The master replied, "I'm going straight to hell."
The puzzled student asked, "Why?"
The master replied, "Because that's where I'll be needed most."

Fleet Maull didn't die in prison, though that was certainly within the realm of possibility. Yet he's intimate with the hell of it. He did his time, found the ground beneath his being, and put it into words. He's here to walk you through the hell realm because that's where he is needed most. Read on—you won't regret it.

Michael O'Keefe is an actor, filmmaker, writer, and longtime Zen practitioner. See www.michaelokeefe.com

Dharma in Hell

Chapter 1
DHARMA IN HELL

Practicing in Prisons and Charnel Grounds

In some ways imprisonment provides a ideal setting for meditation practice similar to a monastery or ashram—simple living, regimented schedule, and so on. But a more accurate analogy for prison spiritual practice might be to compare it to *charnel ground practice.*

Charnel grounds are Indian and Tibetan cemeteries for the poor where traditionally yogis have gone to meditate on death and impermanence. Bodies of the dead are taken to charnel grounds and left in the open air to decompose and be devoured by wild animals. The phrase '*charnel ground*' has become a metaphor to describe practicing in hellish or difficult situations. Prisons, jails, mental institutions, homeless shelters, the streets, urban ghettos, violent homes, war zones, refugee camps, or even living with a

21

painful illness, could all be considered opportunities for charnel ground practice.

In India and Nepal, cremation is the accepted method of disposing of the remains of the dead. This involves purchasing wood and making arrangements with those who perform cremations as a profession. The expenses involved in this are often too much for the poor. So, if a family lacks the means to cremate their loved one's body, they are left with no other recourse than to abandon the corpse in a charnel ground.

Charnel grounds tend be located in relatively remote places, far from towns or villages. So, those who died in disgrace or have been banished by society, such as criminals, taboo breakers, suicides, unmarried or childless women, adulterers, and so on— would often be denied religious rites and cremation, and thus find their way to the charnel grounds.

In Indian folklore, charnel grounds are known to be haunted by jackals and wild beasts who prey on corpses, as well as harmful spirits, demons and vampires. These spirits include the *vetalas* (evil or hostile ghosts of the dead who can take possession of recently deceased corpses); *rakshasas* (vampiric demons living in charnel grounds who prey on infants and small children); *pisachas* (vampiric spirits of a lower order who haunt charnel grounds and crossroads, and cause illness); *bhutas* (troublesome spirits of executed criminals, suicides, or the disgraced who weren't allowed religious funeral rites); and *churnels* (ghosts of women who died in childbirth or broke religious taboos).

Yogis who were determined to liberate themselves—especially from their addiction to physical form—have for several thousand years sought out charnel grounds as an ideal places to practice. Among the decaying corpses they could directly confront their fear of death and the unknown and let go of deeply ingrained attachments. These yogins would construct crude meditation huts among the human remains, even fashioning meditation seats from piles of human bones. The charnel ground became the setting for tantric practice and ritual, where ordinary conventions and taboos were challenged in service of spiritual liberation. Yogins played ritual music on bone trumpets and skull drums. These symbolic instruments were a testament to overcoming attachment to physical form and conquering fear of death.

In Tibetan art, images of tantric buddhas which represent pure states of being are often shown wearing skull crowns and bone ornaments and standing on corpses. This symbolizes the transcendence of ego or self-grasping. These images visually display the transformation of ordinary attachments and emotions into their enlightened nature. Frequently they are pictured inside mandalas (*palaces or abodes*) which are surrounded by a protective circle of charnel grounds serving both as places of practice, and, as deterrents to the timid, impure, or unprepared.

CHARNEL GROUND PRACTICE

In the *Sutra's*, which are the scriptures of Buddha's teachings, monks are encouraged to contemplate the true nature of the body. In "The Nine Charnel Ground Contemplations[1]," it is stated:

> (1) And further, monks, if a monk sees a body dead one, two, or three days; swollen, blue and festering, thrown in the charnel ground, he then applies this perception to his own body thus: "Verily, also my own body is of the same nature; such it will become and will not escape it."

And further on:

> (2) And further, monks, if a monk sees a body thrown in the charnel ground, being eaten by crows, hawks, vultures, dogs, jackals or by different kinds of worms, he then applies this perception to his own body thus: "Verily, also my own body is of the same nature; such it will become and will not escape it."

Here the Buddha tells monks to imagine themselves in a charnel ground, where their bodies are being torn apart and eaten by wild animals. The Buddha disapproved of ascetic practice as a norm, but did approve of thirteen specific actual ascetic practices or *dhutagas*, for practitioners, as long as the practice was not harmful to their temperament. The eleventh of these dhutagas is the vow of living in a charnel ground. The vow is broken if the monk is anywhere other than a charnel ground at the break of dawn each day. Living in a conventional cemetery is not sufficient to practice this dhutaga, as the point is to remain in close contact with decomposing corpses.

In chapter eight entitled "The Perfection of Meditation" of the *Bodhicaryavatara, A Guide to the Bodhisattva's Way of Life*[2] states:

> 30. When shall I go to the local charnel grounds and compare my own body, which has the nature of decay, with other corpses?

> 31. For this body of mine will also become so putrid that even jackals will not come near it because of the stench.

> 32. If the flesh and bone that have arisen together with this body will deteriorate and disperse, how much more is the case for other friends?

> 70. If you are repelled upon seeing just skeletons in a charnel ground, why are you attracted to a village, which is a charnel ground crowded with animated skeletons?

The phrase "a charnel ground crowded with animated skeletons," apart from being an apt description of jails, prisons, and mental institutions, reminds me of the way Gurdjieff described the completely mechanical nature of our non-awakened human existence and the experience of walking about in public and sensing oneself surrounded by the robot-like, walking dead.

Padmasambhava, the great tantric yogin, saint and magician of 8th century Indian Buddhism, played a key role in establishing Vajrayana Buddhism in Tibet, where he is revered as a Buddha and known as Guru Rinpoche. Early in his life, Padmasambhava was held responsible for the death of a minister's son and banished to a charnel ground where he lived and practiced for many years, perfecting his realization and subjugating all the inner and outer demons of the place as well as those within his own mind.

In Tibet, the practice of *sky burial* is found today. There the bodies of commoners (cremation is reserved for lamas or Buddhist teachers and other prominent people) are taken to charnel grounds where professional funeral butchers cut up the corpses and feed the flesh and bones to waiting vultures. Regular folk would never visit such a terrifying place except to witness the disposition of a family member's remains. But Tibetan yogis have long sought out these places to contemplate death and impermanence.

In her essay, "Transformation of the Wolf Man,[3]" Eleanor Rosch tells a traditional story of one such yogin from the Tibetan Buddhist tradition:

Shalipa was a low-caste woodcutter who lived near the charnel ground of Bighapur. Packs of wolves came by night to eat the corpses. The wolves howled all night long, and Shalipa became more and more afraid of them until he could neither eat by day nor sleep by night for fear of the howling of wolves. One evening a wandering yogin stopped by his cottage asking for food. Shalipa gave him food and drink, and, well pleased, the yogin repaid him with a discourse on the virtues of fearing *samsara* (conditioned existence) and practicing the dharma. Shalipa thanked him but said, 'Everyone fears samsara. But I have a specific fear. Wolves come to the charnel ground and howl all night, and I am so afraid of them that I can neither eat nor sleep nor practice the dharma. Please can't you give me a spell so that I can stop the howling of the wolves?' The yogin laughed and said, 'Foolish man. What good will it do you to eat the food of greed when you do not know what food is? What good will it do you to sleep the corpse-like sleep of ignorance when you do not know what rest is? What good will it do you to destroy the howling of the wolves with the spells or anger when you do not know what hearing or any other sense is? If you will follow my instructions, I will teach you to destroy all fear.' Shalipa accepted the yogin

27

as his teacher, gave him all that he had, and begged him for instructions. After giving him initiation, the yogin told him to move into the charnel ground with the wolves and to meditate ceaselessly upon all sound as identical to the howling of wolves. Shalipa obeyed him. Gradually he came to understand the nature of all sound and of all reality. He meditated for nine years, overcame all obscurations of his mind and body, lost all fear, and attained great realization. Thereafter, he wore a wolf skin around his shoulders and was known as *Shalipa* (the wolf yogin). He taught his disciples many different practices about the nature of appearances and reality. He taught the unity of appearance, emptiness, wisdom, and skillful means. Finally, in that very body, he went to the realm of Heroes.[4]

Shalipa's story could have been the story of almost any one of my fellow prisoners during my fourteen-year journey in the charnel grounds known as the U.S. Medical Center for Federal Prisoners in Springfield, Missouri. The men there were mostly poor and under-educated. Many had been forced by poverty and race to live in highly toxic surroundings of one kind or another—next to toxic waste dumps; next to freeways, trains, and subways; or the midst of family chaos and violence driven by alcohol and drugs. Most came from the places reserved for the poor, the marginalized—the lower castes of our supposedly egalitarian society. These men had found themselves living behind bars without the benefit of dharma teachings amidst the howling of wolves. They ended up in prison generally as a result of responding to their situation in the only way they knew, after years of being caught in the ignorance, greed, and aggression of human conditioning.

While my background was certainly more privileged than most of my fellows, my experience of incarceration was no less a charnel ground, no less a direct confrontation with my greatest fears. And like Shalipa, I *had* studied dharma teachings, and I had been accepted and initiated by an accomplished, realized yogin—Tibetan teacher Chogyam Trungpa Rinpoche. Great, good fortune indeed!

My incarceration began with the slamming of the heavy steel cell door in a county jail. There, I awaited my trial. If convicted, I would be sent to federal prison for many years, possibly for life. Apart from the concrete floor, this ten-man cell block was a continuous sheath of welded-steel—the ceiling, the walls, the bunks, toilets—everything. There were no windows, just a meal slot in the steel door. There were five tiny two-man cells—all in a row—facing a narrow open area dominated by a long steel picnic table, where we ate and played cards. In the corner was a very nasty single shower. There wasn't room to walk more three or four paces in the narrow space between the long table and the

29

shower and the row of cells. During the day our cell doors were open. At night we were locked in our cells—lights out at 10pm.

The cellblock was always full, and my cellmates were mostly poor African American men from the inner city slums of St. Louis. They were jailed for all kinds of offenses—drugs, robbery, car theft, murder. One was awaiting trial for killing a state trooper. He was actually a state prisoner, but they couldn't house him with the state prisoners in the other cellblocks which contained mainly 'good ol' boys' from all-white areas of southern Missouri. These 'good ol' boys' had a predilection for beating nearly to death anyone they didn't like. So he was housed with us in the federal cellblock where he would be safe. The authorities wanted to keep him alive for trial and most likely, eventual execution. I was probably safer in the federal cellblock too, although my cellmates let me know in no uncertain terms that my days of "white privilege" were a thing of the past. This was *their* world and I'd best keep my mouth shut if I wanted to get along.

The dominant feature of my county jail experience was noise— outer and inner noise—24 hours a day. Unusual by most jail standards, prisoners were allowed to have portable televisions and radios in their cells if someone on the outside would supply it. So, we had three or four of each going full-blast 24 hours a day. These guys seemed to have a real dislike for anything that approached silence. There was a crew that got up early to watch cartoons, another group that watched game shows and soap operas all day, and the night owls that stayed up all night watching movies and talking shop—recounting their war stories from life in streets. On top of this, there was constant arguing and yelling going on, especially in the other cellblocks on the other side of the corridor.

Loud as all this was, it was mere background noise for the barrage of inner noise—racing thoughts and fears—that plagued me day and night, but especially at night, with the lights out and nothing to read, nothing to do, but lay there. My attention vacillated between the inner and outer chaos, and contemplating a life in prison. One of the counts I was charged with, *Continuous Criminal Enterprise*, the so-called "kingpin statute," carried a minimum sentence of ten years without parole and a maximum of life. The authorities had assured my lawyer of their intent to put me away for at least 30 years. My mind would race back and forth across the events leading to my indictment and arrest, madly searching for a way out, a way this hellish fate could have been avoided. Or my mind would be flooded with a limitless array of escape plans and fantasies, some quite violent. In the darkest moments, I would think of my son and his mother and what I had done to them—how I had abandoned them in a cloud of shame.

If I was tired or sleepy enough at just the right moment, a brief interlude of relative quiet before the late night crowd started exchanging war stories, yelling back and forth from cell to cell, I sometimes fell asleep and found some relief until the lights came on at 6am. But more often than not, sleep eluded me, and my

31

mind raced on. So, along with everything else, I was suffering from sleep deprivation. Several times, desperate for sleep, I had the audacity to suggest turning the TV's down a little. The first couple of times, my request was met with disdain, laughter and vulgarity. My last attempt almost lead to an altercation when five of my cellmates confronted me.

"We know who you are and where you come from. We know you're used to being the center of your world, with everything going your way. You'd better wake up and realize that's all over with. You're in our world now, and you ain't runnin' shit, except your mouth, and that's gonna get you in a lot of trouble. We don't want to hear nothin' from you, nothin' about what you want. You better just shut the fuck up!"

This was the last thing I wanted to hear, but I knew they were right. On the one hand, I thought I had made my requests as gently and politely as one could and their statement that I had so much control in "my world" seemed quite an exaggeration, but the more I thought about it, I knew they were right-on. I gave up. I could be a scrapper when the chips were down, but even the part of me that didn't want to admit they were right wasn't inclined to take on the whole cell.

Also, at this time, I was plagued by nightmares. Between the stories I heard from my cellmates who had been to the penitentiary and all the prison movies I'd seen, my mind imagined the very worst. These were violent nightmares of physical and sexual assaults, gangs, weapons, and even the possibility of having to kill to survive.

Thus began my prison education, with this first encounter with a reality more imposing than my own will. These were my first small steps toward surrendering my view of how things *should* be. Here I'd have to learn how to live in a world where I didn't enjoy privilege or the power of race and class that still predominates outside the prison walls. Of course, my greatest fear was of becoming victimized, and losing my dignity or even my life in a violent attack. I knew deep inside that there were some things I just wouldn't let happen, not without a hell of a fight—but where was I to draw the line? And where did the slippery slope of victimization begin? I didn't realize then that this would be a path of ever deepening discernment that would span my entire journey behind bars.

I related this story of being confronted by my jailmates to one of my teachers, Osel Tendzin (*dharma heir of Chogyam Trungpa*), when he visited me in federal prison years later. I told him how I had eventually given in, and as a result had made friends and found some degree of acceptance with my jailmates. The story reminded him of the renowned Tibetan yogi Milarepa's encounter with the demons who took over his meditation cave and resisted every artifice he employed to get rid of them. The point, of course, wasn't that my cellmates were demons, any more than the ones who appeared in Milarepa's cave were, or that my practice bore any resemblance to Milarepa's, but rather that the similar

33

unrelenting tenacity and resistance of my cellmates prevented any lack of genuineness on my part. Milarepa finally surrendered and made friends with his demons welcoming them as guests. I also learned to surrender and make friends with my jailmates and my environment, though in my case, the challenge was learning how to behave as a gracious guest.

After seven months in the county jail, I received a thirty-year, no-parole sentence. I was then transferred to the federal prison hospital in Missouri. I went from a cell block housing ten prisoners to a correctional facility with over 1,300 prisoners. It was both a relief and frightening to find myself in this much bigger more chaotic environment. The prison population consisted of 300 in general population, or work cadre (prisoners like myself who were there to work in food service, housekeeping, sanitation, or maintenance), and 1,000 hospital patients—approximately 600 medical and 400 psychiatric.

During the first week there, as I oriented myself to my new home, I quickly found that I'd landed in a place of unbelievable suffering. I saw men ravaged by cancer and AIDS, paraplegics and quadriplegics in wheelchairs, and blind men feeling their way down a prison corridor. I saw highly disturbed mental health patients mumbling to themselves or shuffling down the hall with the characteristic step and vacant stare produced by heavy doses of psychotropic drugs used more for purposes of control—so-called *chemical straightjackets*—than for any actual treatment, much less healing. And I had yet to see the locked medical wards or the locked back wards of the psychiatric wing, the infamous 10-building Jack Abbott wrote about in his book, *In the Belly of the Beast.*

I had many years to become intimate with this charnel ground, populated with a pantheon of troubled spirits, vetalas, rakshasa, and the like, rivaling that of Indian folklore. And they weren't all prisoners. Some of the most troubled and troublesome, and some of the scariest charnel ground denizens wore prison guard uniforms. Working in the prison school (*my day job*) for 13 plus years, I helped bitter and angry men—made even angrier by forced enrollment in school—learn to read, pass their high school equivalency (GED) exam, or complete college correspondence courses. I worked with inner city gang members, Asians, African Americans, and Chicanos, with Mexican rancheros imprisoned for drug dealing or immigration violations. I worked with mental health patients who could make a little progress on their "good" days, until one of the prison psychiatrists started experimenting with their meds again.

I was determined to keep my heart open in this hell realm of incalculable pain, anger, bitterness, anguish and depression. I knew that spiritual practice and study were key and I devoted myself to these disciplines with vigor.

Early on in my prison journey, I began to follow the work of social activist Bernie Glassman, a traditionally trained western Zen master who was working to alleviate suffering among the poorest of the poor and the homeless. He had developed an innovative new model for addressing seemingly intractable social ills through a holistic approach to community development. In 1994, I began formal studies with Roshi Glassman, or "Bernie" as he prefers to be called these days, which eventually led to my ordination as a Zen peacemaker priest in a ceremony performed in the prison chapel by Roshi and his late wife, Sensei Jishu.

Bernie and Jishu founded the Zen Peacemaker Order and the Peacemaker Community which are known for *plunge* practices such as *street retreats* and the annual *Bearing Witness* retreat at Auschwitz-Birkenau (site of one of the largest Nazi death camps). These plunges are essentially deep journeys' into charnel grounds, where all reference points quickly dissolve, plunging the retreatant into the depths of *not knowing*, the first tenet of the Peacemaker Community approach to spiritually-based social action (the other two tenets are *bearing witness* and *loving action*).

Since leaving prison in 1999, I have found myself irresistibly drawn to these plunge practices. I've attended the street retreats in New York City with Bernie, led street retreats myself in Denver yearly, and spent time sitting between the railroad tracks at the infamous *selection site* at Birkenau. Here the Jews, gypsies and other "undesirables," were rounded up by the Nazi's and taken from the cattle cars and directed to the left or to the right—to immediate extermination in the gas chambers, or, to a slower death in the slave labor camps.

Bernie Glassman had visited Auschwitz-Birkenau in the early 1990's, experiencing a realm of suffering spirits who were starving for recognition, remembrance, healing and release. He vowed to return there in an effort to bring healing to these displaced and forgotten beings. In 1996, he returned with 150 like-minded and courageous peacemakers seeking healing for the souls of Auschwitz-Birkenau, for their families, communities, nations, and for humanity.

In the extremely cold Polish November weather, an interfaith community of peacemakers from many different countries sits together in meditation. We take turns reading the names of the dead—those few whose names are known—and bear witness to the unspeakable horror of the place where millions of men, women, and children—the majority Jews, but also Polish Catholics, Russian soldiers, gypsies, homosexuals, and other so-called "undesirables"—were systematically exterminated. The dead were burned in the crematoria and open fields of this death camp and charnel ground, which is now a vast cemetery, a repository of the ashes of nearly two million human beings.

The visible corpses are now long gone, almost sixty years after the Russian soldiers liberated the camp in 1945. But their spirits and anguish linger—not only in the horrific visual images preserved in the camps and museums—but also in the stories told by the camp survivors and children of camp survivors who join us each year on the retreat.

37

Why am I drawn to continue practicing in charnel grounds even after my release from prison? Why do peacemakers return year after year to bear witness individually and with each other to the horrors of Auschwitz-Birkenau, this monument to the dark side of human nature? The question is difficult to answer.

One reason I'm drawn to these charnel-ground-like practices is that they simply accentuate what we all deal with day-in and day-out in our lives. In this type of practice I am able to bring mindfulness and awareness to the suffering of the world and bear witness to it. We all experience charnel grounds in our lives. Especially between our ears, where the "rush hour"-like traffic of discursive thinking, conflicting emotions, raging desires and aversions is perhaps the ultimate charnel ground, and where our practice comes home to in the end.

Notes

[1.] *The Foundations of Mindfulness, Satipatthana Sutta,* translated by Nyanasatta Thera (Vipassana Fellowship)

[2.] *Bodhicaryavatara*, Shantideva Society and the Bodhicaryavatara Historical Project

[3.] In J. Pickering (ed.) *The Authority of Experience: Essays on Buddhism and Psychology.* Surrey: Curzon Press, 1997

[4.] This version of the Shalipa story is from an oral account by the late Jamgon Kongtrul. Variant written versions can be found in Dowman, K. (1985). *Masters of mahamudra.* Albany, N.Y.: State University of New York Press; and Robinson, J.B. (1979). *Buddha's lions: The lives of the eighty-four siddhas.*

Chapter 2
PRISON MONASTICISM
edited from article in Turning Wheel, *Winter 1992*

The Lama leaned forward from his brocade-covered teaching chair. "So in your letter you said that you wanted to take the novice vows." I nodded my head and briefly explained my reasons. Seemingly satisfied, Rinpoche asked me to kneel in front of the Buddhist shrine that had been set up for the *abhisheka* (empowerment) ceremony to focus my mind on the triple refuge of the Buddha, Dharma and Sangha, and on my aspiration to take and keep the vows. He then snapped his fingers and said, "That's it, you have made your commitment to keep the novice vows." This was November 1989, in the prison chapel at the federal prison where I'd been incarcerated on drug smuggling charges since 1985.

The Venerable Thrangu Rinpoche, abbot of monasteries in Tibet, Sikkim, Nepal, and Nova Scotia, had very generously made a special stop in Springfield to perform the abhisheka ceremony for me during the U.S. leg of a worldwide teaching tour. Since that day, almost two years ago, I have been groping along, trying to discover how to live and practice as a monk in prison.

Several years ago, during a talk by Bill Bothwell, a visiting Buddhist teacher from Los Angeles, a prisoner commented that we could regard our prison situation as a kind of monastic experience. This comparison has been made frequently, and I tend to view my own prison experience in this light. So, I was quite surprised when Bill said, "that's kind of a cute idea—it *could* be helpful. But it could just be more 'thinking'—further conceptualizing of a situation which is actually just as it is." Bill's comment came from a fresh mind with no need to romanticize and it stopped my mind on the spot.

It may be helpful at times to regard prison as a monastery, because this perspective might help you see your imprisonment as a total practice situation and as a potentially beneficial experience. In prison, as in a monastery, one is isolated in a separate community apart from the world. One's life is simplified. There are no bills to pay, and few responsibilities beyond doing what one is told and fulfilling the duties of one's prison job. One is also not involved in family life directly although some prisoners remain connected to the outside by means of correspondence and telephone.

Most prisons, like most monasteries and nunneries, are single-sex environments. However, the staff will most likely be both sexes these days. (At this particular men's prison, over half of the 600 staff people are women.)

But apart from those similarities, prison is nothing like a monastery or any other environment designed for dharma practice, and it could be just a fantasy trip to view it as such. Noise and chaos are a prison's most pervasive qualities. Next come anger and hostility, and finally an anxious boredom and attitude of seeking entertainment and "killing time." There is also a feeling of hopelessness that casts a pall over the prison population, especially during the long winter months when the recreation yards close early.

I once tried to describe what prison was like to a visiting friend who lived in a two-bedroom apartment. I told her "imagine cramming as many bunk-beds as possible into your living room and two bedrooms and then rounding up about fifty or sixty of the loudest, most inconsiderate people you can find to move in with you on a permanent basis."

The noise and lack of privacy are the greatest obstacles to formal meditation practice in prison. From 7am to 11pm, the prison's overcrowded living areas are in constant uproar. Even the quieter times are filled with the sound of "soft rock" music piped in through the public address system. In the evenings, the residential

41

units take on the atmosphere of a nightclub, with loud card and domino games everywhere.

The halls are like busy streets on hot Saturday nights—everybody's hanging out, yelling, hustling. It's difficult to find a place to practice meditation in this chaos. In the large dorms, you can sit on your bunk in the dark, late at night or early in the morning. But, during the day or early evening you have to be able to stand both the noise and everyone looking at you.

To practice during the daytime, I cleaned out one of the sanitation closets where the mops, brooms, and trash barrels are kept. I would set everything outside so that I wouldn't be disturbed, take a chair in, and sit for an hour or two. The noise level was still about the same, but the closet was at least a defined space where I could practice with a little less distraction.

The doors to these closets have a small window, so people would look in. Some people, not seeing that I had set everything outside, would burst in through the door to get a mop, only to be shocked by seeing me sitting there. During the summer my trash closet meditation cell was like a sauna. I would sit with sweat pouring down my face, into my eyes, everywhere. Looking back, I am amazed that I stuck with it.

I practiced in the closet for several years before I was moved to a single room. Some weekend days I would even manage four or five hours of sitting practice. This "in-the-closet" practice was ironically quite public. A lot of people thought I was weird, sitting in the trash closet, but they got used to it. I have often recommended this option to other prisoners, but I only know of one who ever tried it. Most people are just too self-conscious to practice so publicly. After, when I had a single room, if someone on my unit needed to practice, I encouraged them to use my room while I was at work.

Prison chapel facilities could be ideal places for formal sitting practice, but unfortunately their use is very tightly scheduled to meet the demands of numerous religious practitioners: Christian, Muslim, Jewish, Native American, and others. The staff and the chapel tend to be dominated by Christian—especially fundamentalist Christian—values and programming. It is not uncommon to encounter prison chaplains who regard Buddhism as a foreign or even dangerous cult.

Fortunately, the attitudes are not always that rigid. With some gentle persistence and the help of two other Buddhist prisoners— a young man from Nepal and a middle-aged engineer from Taiwan—I was able to establish a Buddhist meditation group in the chapel. We met each Saturday for an hour. For several years, we would put a few chairs in a circle and sit. Eventually we were able to expand to two hours. Eventually we managed to build a portable Buddhist shrine, and we even acquired a number of meditation cushions.

Finally, the chapel started staying open one additional evening each week, and we were able to obtain another hour for sitting meditation on Wednesday evenings. We developed a sitting and teaching program that was a combination of talks, dharma videos and discussion each Saturday, and just sitting each Wednesday. On the first Saturday of each month, we did a three-hour session of sitting and walking meditation.

The prison I'm in is primarily a medical facility with a transient population, so our group remained small with a constant turnover through the years. One outside Buddhist group in Kansas City was able to provide some support. Though it's a four-to-five hour drive each way and they were very involved keeping their own outside group going amidst the pressures of city life, jobs, and family responsibilities they were able to visit us a few times.

Although it is difficult to do formal practice in prison, the environment may be ideal for an ongoing discipline of mindfulness. Prison is so intense and inescapable that if one has any experience of awareness practice at all, it becomes a constant reflection of one's state of mind, moment-by-moment. Instead of a monastery, the *charnel ground* [*see Chapter 1*] of Indian and Tibetan Buddhism might be a better metaphor for the prison practice environment.

Over the centuries, the charnel ground has become a natural metaphor for any extreme practice situation full of obstacles. It is said that if one can practice under such difficult circumstances, the potential for realization is greatly increased.

I have the utmost respect for prisoners everywhere who make any attempt to practice the dharma. Although Buddhism and meditation are still regarded with indifference and even outright suspicion in most prisons in the United States, we are nonetheless fortunate to be allowed to practice at all. Our dharma brothers and sisters who are political prisoners in a number of Asian countries are forbidden any outward form of dharma practice under penalty of torture and death. That these courageous men and women maintain their inner practice and keep the essence of their vows for years under such adverse circumstances is the greatest inspiration to my own efforts at practice under much easier circumstances.

In the dormitories where most prisoners live, it only takes a few inconsiderate people to make life miserable for everyone else. In most prisons, the large number of informants prevents any kind of organized management by the inmates. One simply has to put up with all the obnoxious behavior or be prepared to fight a lot and do a lot of time in the "hole" (segregation unit). True, one could take the radical approach of intentionally going to the hole for the purpose of doing retreat practice, but even in the hole, the cells are mostly double-occupancy!

I have been fortunate to have one of only four single rooms on a sixty-five-man ward for the last five years I've been in prison. While this provides only partial refuge from the chaos just outside the door, it allowed me to complete the foundational *ngondro* practices of the Kagyu lineage of Tibetan Buddhism and receive an *abhisheka* or empowerment.

Prison room assignments are based on seniority and ability to stay out of trouble. Any kind of infraction of the rules can lead to losing your room and starting over at the bottom of the seniority list. Of course, one could also be transferred to another institution without warning, where one would start all over again in a crowded dorm. This reminder of impermanence has been a great inspiration to practice and also a source of some guilt when I don't practice.

I was fortunate to have a strong foundation in dharma practice before coming to prison. My initial efforts in meditation practice started in 1974. I took refuge vows in 1978 as a student in the Tibetan Buddhist tradition, and completed a Master's Degree in Buddhist and Western Psychology in 1979 at Naropa University.

I would like to relate something here about my past lifestyle as both a drug smuggler and a dharma practitioner. The discontent I felt as a young man in the 1960s led me, like many others, to search for some kind of genuine experience, something beyond the artificiality that seemed to pervade the conventional world.

This search led me into the counterculture and drugs and also toward an exploration of Eastern religions. The former took precedence over the latter for a long time. By the time I began to meditate on my own I had been involved in serious alcohol and drug abuse for many years.

I eventually turned to small-scale smuggling to support an expatriate lifestyle in South America and later to finance moving back to the United States. I wanted to go back to school, and had a new wife who was pregnant. By the time I met my teacher Chogyam Trungpa, and took refuge, I no longer felt the burning political and social alienation of earlier years, but I was profoundly addicted to alcohol, cocaine, and easy money.

For a number of years I led a dual life. One life was lived as an active member of a Buddhist community that encouraged its members to develop sanity in all aspects of their lives. The other life was as a secret smuggler and addict. Friends in the community who knew about my secret life continually encouraged me to leave it behind. Addictions, obviously, are not easy to let go of, and by the time I quit, it was too late to get off unscathed.

Past associations eventually brought about my indictment in May 1985 on multiple charges of smuggling cocaine and conducting an ongoing criminal enterprise. With the encouragement of my teachers and advisors in the Buddhist community, I decided to face the consequences of my past behavior rather than flee the country, even though a long prison sentence was almost a certainty. That is a decision I have never regretted. I am just glad that I finally had developed enough sanity to accept their guidance.

I started sitting daily in a two-man cell in a hellish, overcrowded county jail. There, for seven months, I awaited trial and sentencing, and I have been sitting daily ever since. When I finally acquired a single room in 1987, I was able to begin again the ngondro practices- hundreds of thousands of prostrations and recitations, for which I had received transmission in 1981. I would arise at 3:30am in order to do the practices while it was still quiet.

My room had a door and a small window. People looked in sometimes. The guards would come by to count heads at 5am, they could see me doing full prostrations on the floor beside my bed. In the middle of a session of one thousand prostrations, sweat pouring off me and my heart pounding, I would gasp for breath and feel very shaky, vulnerable, and out of control. It was scary. Generally, these are not the kind of feelings one cultivates in prison—it's just too threatening.

It took me about fifteen months of intense practice, sleeping only four hours a night, to finish ngondro. During that period I also began taking the Five Lay Precepts (*Not Killing, Stealing, Lying, Misusing Sex, or Using Drugs*) formally on a daily basis. Before coming to prison, I had only worked with the precepts briefly in group retreat situations. Other than that, I had ignored them.

I began trying to live by the lay precepts to some extent upon entering federal prison in 1985; however, when I began working with them formally on a daily basis three years later, I found they added a powerful new dimension to my mindfulness practice. What came into focus more than anything else were my habitual patterns of false, harmful and useless speech.

My interest in monastic practice grew and the experience of living by formal precepts led to a strong desire to take novice monastic vows, at least for the duration of my prison time. I wanted to develop a practical and beneficial model of prison monasticism, with the idea of making that model available to other interested prisoners—possibly through a book of some sort, or maybe even in the form of an actual Order for Prison Monks.

Still, I realized that before I could consider any such grandiose ideas, I would have to apply them to myself—"fully and properly" as my teacher, Chogyam Trungpa Rinpoche would often say. So I was happy when Thrangu Rinpoche agreed to let me take temporary novice vows for the duration of my time in prison. Upon release, I would decide whether to continue on a monastic path or return to lay practice.

The novice monk keeps precepts that address three areas of behavior: refraining from actions that may harm others, refraining from actions that may harm oneself, and refraining from actions that distract from the discipline of mindfulness.

While the first two areas are very important, it is in the third area that the environment of the monastic life is developed. This third area is a process of simplifying one's life. My advisor for monastic practice, Pema Chodron, director of Gampo Abbey in Nova Scotia, speaks of this process as "creating an unpainted canvas of our life," where our habitual patterns of egocentric behavior stand out in sharp contrast.

I know from experience that arbitrarily imposing strict discipline on myself normally results in fits of rebelliousness, followed by pangs of guilt and compulsive self-recrimination. This being one of my habitual neurotic scenarios, it seemed best to avoid. So, while making every effort to keep the basic five precepts as purely as possible, the approach I have so far taken with the monastic precepts has been to begin somewhat loosely and then gradually to tighten up through a trial-and-error process of learning what best encourages mindfulness. This way I find that I develop a genuine sense of appreciation for the disciplines and am able to integrate them into my life as something natural and desirable, even as a source of joy, rather than as some kind of externally imposed set of limitations.

It has now been almost two years since I took monastic vows, and it has taken me that long to really commit myself to working with them. I wasn't, of course, allowed to wear monastic robes in prison, so I found it very easy to forget that I was indeed a monk. Nothing in the environment recognized this major life change I had made, so it was a challenge to continually remind myself of it.

I remember that at the time of the vow ceremony, Thrangu Rinpoche had said that my regular prison khakis could suffice for monastic robes and that if shaving my head would be a problem in the prison environment, I could just keep my hair relatively short. He also recommended a moderate meal in the early evening to strengthen my studies in the late evening, even though the traditional practice is not to eat after midday.

Even though it was hard to overcome my habits of compulsive eating and late night snacking, I decided eventually not to eat solid foods past midday. I began to experience a quality of spaciousness through simplifying and it actually became natural. I did take fruit juice in the evenings and even enjoyed a pint of ice cream at 5pm on commissary night, our once-a-week night for shopping at the prison canteen. One shouldn't be too rigid in these matters after all!

Probably as a result of past abuses, I developed a mild inflammation in the duodenum which necessitated taking a light meal in the late afternoon. To my relief though, this didn't cause a resurgence of compulsive eating habits, I didn't feel I was making sacrifices so much as naturally letting go of what was unnecessary.

Of course, I have discovered all this between periods of tenaciously holding on to old ways. It's my way, I suppose to be dragged kicking and screaming into something new, only to discover that I like where I have arrived when I get there.

For example, for months after taking vows I resisted cutting my hair, and when I did cut it short the first time, I let it grow again immediately. I also kept my mustache for awhile. It was hard to give up some degree of normalcy in a strange environment, where many prisoners are into peculiar hair trips, like shaving their heads bald. But a lot of the resistance was just simple vanity and my usual resistance to change. When I finally started keeping my hair very short, I felt a great sense of relief in the discipline and simplicity.

At times I wondered why I was attempting to be a monk in prison. Prison is hard enough without looking for ways to make it harder. Sometimes when I saw others preparing the standard late-night snack of nacho chips and cheese sauce heated in the microwave, I longed for that kind of momentary relief from boredom and loneliness. Sometimes I would just wanted to forget the whole thing, and spend my time hanging out, watching TV or reading novels.

In the midst of such thoughts though, I came back to the reality of how little real satisfaction there is in those things. I remembered how wretched I felt when those activities were the substance of my life. Reflecting on that, the simple and spacious quality of the monastic discipline takes on a refreshing quality. I still have very little idea of what it really means to be a monk in prison, but it was a relief and at times even a great joy just to be alive and practicing the Dharma in prison.

Chapter 3
MONEY & LIVELIHOOD BEHIND BARS

from *Turning Wheel, Summer 1993*

One of my first bunkmates was a cook in the prison kitchen. When I moved in above him, he started working on me right away, trying to sign me up on one of his dinner contracts. Three or four prisoners each paid him several hundred dollars a month for a restaurant-quality meal every evening: steak, chicken, or deluxe hamburger. The meals included salad and dessert, and were served in the cells, with tablecloth and dinnerware. The cook was making serious money by prison standards. I suppose I still had an air of money about me from the street, but I was actually completely broke and already committed to avoiding that kind of prison hustling as much as possible, so he gave up on me after a few days.

Before coming to prison, I didn't think much about the Buddhist practices of *Right Livelihood* or the Lay Precepts. Like many Westerners, I was more interested in the practice of meditation and the Buddhist teachings on the nature of mind. Unfortunately, my spiritual yearnings had long run parallel with my addictions. Yet, my denial was so strong that I was blind to the jarring incongruities in my life.

Even after taking refuge and bodhisattva vows, I continued to engage in criminal activity, without ever experiencing any sense of the wrongness of my career. I began to feel the precariousness of my situation and tried to extricate myself from that way of life, but I still wasn't able to see the harm I had been causing until that first cell door slammed shut and my life unraveled completely.

In the weekly recovery meetings I began to attend in prison, I heard the stories of other addicts and realized the harm I had been doing to others by bringing cocaine into this country. When the coke epidemic hit a few years later, I saw what a devastating effect cocaine (my pre-prison livelihood) was capable of having on whole communities. It became very clear to me that I needed to make the practice of *Right Livelihood* [work that benefits rather than harms others] a central focus of my training from that point on.

In federal prison the authorities try to equalize prisoners as much as possible and to keep a lid on all the smuggling and black-marketering that goes on by limiting what people can spend.

There is a commissary where you can shop once a week for postage stamps, pens, notebooks, toiletry items, laundry soap, beverages, snack food, athletic shoes and sweat suits. You can also buy a small Walkman style radio with headphones, an inexpensive watch, or a small fan to provide some relief during the hot summer months. You pay for your purchases with a plastic, magnetic-strip account card, which also serves as a picture I.D.

While there is no limit on the amount of money you can have in your commissary account, you are only allowed to spend up to $125 a month. You can also purchase up to $15 a week in coins to use in the washing machines, dryers, and vending machines on the residential units, but you're not allowed to have any more than $20 in coins in your possession at any time. If you're caught with more than that, you'll lose the money, and you may do some time in the hole as well. At the very least, you will lose your room seniority, which means starting out again on a top bunk in one of the large, noisy dormitories. Still, men who carry a lot of coins find ways to hide them, or stash them with other prisoners.

The $125 a month spending limit serves mainly to limit an individual's use of outside resources. Most prisoners have no money coming in from the outside, and wages range from $11 to $60 a month for full-time prison jobs, but most of the prisoners make less than $25 a month, and many, especially the medical and psychiatric patients who account for two-thirds of the population at this institution, earn only $4 a month for part-time work, or nothing at all. Some prisoners look to some kind of honest but *gray-market* work like washing and ironing clothes, cleaning rooms, or cutting hair for other prisoners. Some make greeting cards, draw portraits, or produce arts and crafts to sell to augment their income. Many resort to food smuggling or some other hustle to get money. Some even manage to send money home to their families!

One can get by with no money in prison. The institution provides you with three meals a day, work clothing, and basic toiletry items. You can throw your prison-issue clothing, which is stamped with your name and bin number, in the laundry cart, and it will reappear several days later in your clothing room bin. Socks and towels can be exchanged daily in the clothing room for clean ones.

Being broke in prison is kind of a drag though. You feel somehow disempowered by not being able to buy things, which in our culture seems to be the ultimate mark of personhood. But you are not looked down on for being broke in prison, as long as you don't become a mooch—always borrowing or asking for things from others. Some men do adjust to living with very little, even some who were doing quite well on the street. Most, however, try to get money somehow.

I've lived very simply in the past, especially during my early traveling years, when all my earthly possessions fit easily into a backpack. That's actually one aspect of prison life that was enjoyable for me—just learning to live simply again. My temporary novice monastic vows further reinforced the idea of keeping things simple. I always tried to ask myself whether I really needed something. But, my small locker space, almost entirely taken up with books and correspondence files, provided a built-in limitation.

I didn't really have to struggle for money. My family sent me funds since my fourth month in, so I can't really speak about what it's like to be destitute in prison for any length of time. I probably spent about 75 percent of what I earned and what my family sent on postage for my extensive correspondence, and on phone calls to my son who lives in South America. The rest went for toiletries and food items. Once a year or so, I bought a new pair of tennis shoes. At Christmas I bought a lot of holiday food items in the commissary and threw an extended party for prison friends and neighbors.

For those who have the money, there is a flourishing black market in food smuggled out of the prison kitchen and in stolen clothing issue, especially new socks, underwear and towels. Also, if you have the money, you can eat better on your residential unit than you can in the dining hall. You can buy three-inch thick, deli-style sandwiches, real hamburgers, omelet sandwiches, and sometimes burritos for 75 cents to a dollar; or you could buy tomatoes, green peppers, onions, and cheese to cook up a batch of classic, prison-style nachos. They sell the chips in the commissary.

I even saw homemade pizza smuggled out of the kitchen. They would precook the dough in the kitchen, and then finish cooking the pizza with toppings to order in the newly installed microwaves in the residential units. Before that, all cooking in the units was done with stolen heat lamps. A friend of mine used to run a grill in his room every night preparing hamburgers to order with a cookie tin and a heat lamp.

Prisoners are not permitted to give each other anything of value, so all the business that goes on violates policy and is subject to punishment. But it's just impossible to control, and prisoners routinely buy and sell anything of value, barter goods and services, loan each other money, and gamble on sports and card games. The media of exchange are coins, books of postage stamps, cigarettes, and commissary items.

Larger debts, primarily from gambling or jailhouse lawyer fees, are settled outside the prison by having family or friends send funds back and forth and into prisoners' commissary accounts. Gambling is the major evening entertainment in prison, and for some it's a livelihood. At about 7pm the gambling enthusiasts transform the TV rooms into casinos, where they play poker until lights out.

Despite all the hustling, the efforts made by prison authorities to keep prisoners on relatively equal footing, both socially and economically, are largely successful, which is a good thing. Even a prisoner with unlimited financial resources can't really live much better than any other prisoner in federal prison. You can only wear so many athletic shoes and jogging suits, and you can only eat so many black market sandwiches.

Shortly after arriving, I found a job in the prison education department where I felt I would be able to earn an honest wage while using some of my talents and education to help others. I worked full-time, teaching prisoners to read and helping them to prepare for the GED exam. I enjoyed this work and felt good about it. As the senior tutor, I earned about $60 a month.

Knowing I was extremely fortunate for the help my family gave me, I never felt judgmental toward those who hustle to get by, and I have a lot of respect for the men who find ways to earn and send money home to their needy families. But it saddens me greatly that the system is set up so that prisoners are actually encouraged to become proficient at hustling and thievery while in prison, skills that will only lead to more crime and more prison time down the road.

It was difficult to avoid participating in the black market completely. Like it or not, the convict world was my community, and I often found myself trying to balance my commitment to the precepts with the Buddhist vows I have taken to help others.

Something as simple as a birthday party for a friend is bound to involve some black market food. Prison-style nachos were the usual fare. I must confess to having bought a few black market pizzas which were pretty good! But, I split them with a hospice patient, probably so I wouldn't feel guilty.

At work I sometimes assisted my students with very simple legal work, like writing a letter to the parole board, but I always refused payment. I decided very early on that I didn't want to profit from helping my fellow prisoners.

Many prisoners often asked for help with legal work, probably because they thought I was educated. There were times when my son and his mother's living situation in South America was really bad. During those times I was tempted to get into the jailhouse lawyer business to help. Each time though, after considerable agonizing and pride swallowing, I instead reached out to my parents and friends in the outside Buddhist community for help. This meant breaking a deeply ingrained pattern of refusing to ask for help and looking for a way to make a quick buck instead. So this was a positive change for me, and I know it's been better for my son, too. My family and friends were incredibly generous. My family provided my son with ongoing support, and a group of Buddhist friends raised the money for him to visit me and then go on to Nova Scotia to participate in a youth program called Sun Camp.

Another important part of right livelihood practice involves the way I related to the people I worked with, both the prisoners and the staff. Prisoners and staff generally have an adversarial relationship. The staff expects the prisoners to steal and let a certain amount of it go, in many cases, as a kind of job perk in order to keep good workers, especially in the kitchen and on the hospital wards.

I've always tried to be honest with my work supervisors, as far as my own behavior was concerned, and I tried to do a good job. I also tried to support my coworkers and be sensitive to the needs of my students. The education staff respects that and so do many of the prisoners. Even though many try to get by with as little work as possible, they do respect someone who does a good job, as long as he's careful to be a prisoner first and not act like a staff person. The fact that my job involved helping prisoners also earned respect.

Sometimes other prisoners would ask me to steal office supplies. My bosses generally gave me whatever I needed for my own use, so I usually just gave them something from my own supplies. When they pressed me for bigger quantities that would have to be stolen, I told them I didn't do that, I usually explained that it wasn't worth risking my job, but sometimes if the person seemed open, I'd share something about my monastic commitments.

Hardly anyone sees stealing from the institution as immoral. Prisoners see it more as liberating things from the enemy, or just trying to get even. Even some of the more religious Christian prisoners I know don't regard stealing from the institution as a problem. For me though, it's not so much a moral issue as it is a question of discipline, having to do with the qualities I would like to cultivate in myself, and thievery and smuggling are just not among those qualities.

I understand why many prisoners feel obligated to fight back in any way they can against the injustices of our prison system, and how they see stealing as part of that struggle, but, unfortunately, this approach is mainly self-destructive. I've given a lot of thought to how prisons could be set up differently, to build self-esteem and encourage the development of ethical principles like *Right Livelihood*, rather than just cultivating bitterness, anger, and thievery. Maybe one day I will get the chance to implement some of those ideas somewhere. But sometimes I would just as soon see all prisons torn down, since in their present form they are horrible places not fit for human habitation.

Chapter 4

DEATH WITHOUT DOGMA

from Shambhala Sun, March 1995

"God bless you . . . and God bless your family," Buck yelled after me in his strained, endearing voice as I left the room. I stopped and said, "God bless you Buck, and your family too."

As a Buddhist, I found saying "God bless you" a little awkward at first, but later it became a natural part of my routine. Buck's God Bless You was all heart. He *meant* it, his voice often full of emotion. I meant it too, though perhaps with a little different understanding.

Working with men of different faiths—primarily theistic and God-centered beliefs—has been one of the most interesting and challenging dimensions of hospice volunteer work.

At times I struggled with the conceptual conflicts that arose doing interfaith work. I wanted to be genuine and of benefit to my patients, as well as remain true to myself.

There were many times when it was not a problem. Times when all conceptual differences fell away and a simple heart-to-heart, being-to-being communication arose. There is a mutual recognition of the profundity and sacredness of life and death that needs no special language, and sometimes no words at all.

The basics of prison hospice caregiving are fairly simple. During the course of a patient's illness, we provide whatever physical or domestic assistance he needs and try to just *be* there for him. We provide moral support and understanding as a close friend or family member might do on the outside. A critical element is helping patients avoid the negative or self-destructive reactions they often have to the callousness and brutality that pervades prisons.

We try to help patients explore their own resources and look for ways to enhance the quality of life and add meaning and richness to the time they have left. If patients are willing to work on healing personal or family situations or other unfinished business, we help with that as well.

Once the actual dying process begins—a stage lasting from just a few days to several weeks—caregiving centers mainly around physical pain or discomfort and fear. We focus on doing whatever we can to keep the patient comfortable and lessen their fear.

This is frequently the time when patients begin to voice religious or spiritual concerns and to make requests for prayer and pastoral services. I remember reading about a woman who was doing interfaith ministry to the dying. She recounted how a mentor had challenged her to transcend her personal religious identifications in order to join her patients wholeheartedly in prayer and spiritual communion. I'd begun to see that this was the kindest approach for me to take as well with my own hospice work.

Early in my hospice work, I avoided praying with patients or using the terminology and concepts of faiths I didn't share, even the Roman Catholicism of my childhood. I've always been willing to read the Bible or other spiritual works for my patients, but I drew the line at praying. For that, I would call on one of the chaplains or another hospice volunteer of the appropriate faith.

There was a time, however, when I found myself in a situation where no outside help was available. It was just me and the patient—by then he was a good friend near death—who needed someone to pray with him. I held his hand and we prayed together. After that, I was in similar situations many times. Each time I found myself responding differently, and with a greater or lesser sense of ease.

Over time though, I found that being a Buddhist practitioner with a nontheistic, almost secular, understanding of spirituality, provided a good foundation for this kind of interfaith ministry. Buddhism has a non-dogmatic and experiential approach to life and death, and accepts the reality of impermanence. Buddhism also addresses something fundamental—an unconditional basic goodness (*buddhanature*) that patients easily recognize and understand.

RAUL . . .

One of my hospice patients, Raul, was a Mexican national in his mid-fifties. He had recently been sent for the first time to prison, where he was diagnosed with terminal cancer in his stomach and lungs. He had been a powerful, commanding figure before falling ill—the head of two families—one in Mexico, one in the U.S. His life had fallen apart quickly and because of this he was very angry. I had a hard time connecting with Raul. I often wondered why he wanted a hospice volunteer at all. He actually had a friend on his ward, another patient, who was already fulfilling that role, so I wondered why he needed me, since he didn't seem to want me in his world. A lack of welcoming a hospice worker was something we rarely experienced from patients in prison hospice work.

Prisoners get an annual vacation from their prison jobs. During my own vacation I wanted to take advantage of my single room to do an intensive meditation retreat. On the first day of my ten-day vacation retreat, I was interrupted by a guard who told me I was needed immediately on the cancer ward: Raul had taken a turn for the worse.

For the next five days, I sat for four to five hours each day at the bedside of this angry man with whom I was barely on speaking terms. In the past, he had often sent me away when I came to visit. Now—in this time of crisis—it was clear that I was welcome, and that I had a job to do.

Raul was barely able to speak. Even though he was receiving morphine orally and intravenously, he was in extreme pain. His need to spit out phlegm would wake him every few minutes.

I sat with him, observing his breathing as well as my own, contemplating death. Whenever he awoke, I would help him sit up to spit into the green plastic basin I kept clean for him. The intimacy of one human being caring for another transcended whatever kept us from connecting before. When Raul was anxious, I would encourage him to slow his breathing. He could manage a word or two to let me know he was in pain, but otherwise our communication was just being together.

With Raul, I didn't need to deal with religious or spiritual issues. His friend on the ward, a Native American cancer patient, had been taking care of that, as well as talking to Raul's family on the phone. Another Hispanic patient spent a lot of time with him, silently saying a Rosary.

Accompanying Raul to the end, I focused on attending to his comfort, which seems to be the essence of caregiving—spiritual or otherwise—especially when the patient is in the throes of dying.

CLARENCE . . .

"Clarence, can you hear me?" Clarence, so big that his body took up the full length of the bed and then some, stirred a little and half opened his eyes. His breathing was shallow and somewhat labored. "Hello Clarence. I'm one of the hospice volunteers. The chaplain talked to you about me coming up to visit you, didn't he?"

Clarence nodded, but didn't look too sure about it. The prison chaplain had told me that Clarence was a Buddhist. Since I was the only Buddhist hospice volunteer, I was assigned to him. He appeared to be quite drowsy from his medication. He had advanced lung cancer and wasn't expected to live long. For a man dying of cancer, he still had a huge, seemingly robust body. His breathing was labored—not yet the rapid, shallow breathing that often precedes death.

I mentioned that I was Buddhist. No sign of recognition crossed his face. I asked the chaplain about it later, and he insisted Clarence had a connection with Buddhism. I didn't bring it up in our next few visits. At this point Clarence was barely responsive. He would sometimes open his eyes and look at me, but mostly he would just lie there struggling to breathe.

One day I brought him a postcard of a traditional statue of the Buddha, just to see if there was any reaction or recognition. Nothing. I felt very uncomfortable. This man is probably a devout Baptist or something, and here I am, waving a picture of the Buddha in his face! After that I just dropped the issue of Clarence's religious persuasion, and focused on providing comfort and alleviating fear.

I was with Clarence for about five hours on the evening he died. The staff provided me with a reclining chair, normally used for chemotherapy. Usually it's hard to find even a metal folding chair. I put the recliner next to his bed, and settled in for the duration.

I knew that Clarence was close to death. It was obvious from the changes in his breathing, eye color, and skin tone. I alternated observing his breathing and heartbeat (which was clearly visible beneath the skin of his now shrunken chest), encouraging him to breathe easy, to relax, and not be afraid, wiping his brow with a cool cloth; practicing mindfulness of breath meditation, and silently reading a meditation book.

Whenever Clarence got particularly anxious, struggling and gasping to breathe, I did a co-breathing meditation with him, asking him to listen to and breathe with the sound of my voice as I vocalized a long, slow out-breath: "Aaaaah," and then another. His breathing slowed down dramatically and his muscles visibly relaxed. I used this technique with many of my patients during their final hours, and have learned to trust its power and effectiveness.

A change in Clarence's breathing alerted me to the approaching moment of his death. I sat up a bit and adjusted my own breathing to the general rhythm of his. I took a moment to tune in further, confirming my sense that he was at the brink of death, and then I spoke to him softly. I told him that the moment of his death had arrived and that there was nothing to fear; he could just let go and be at peace. With that, his breathing slowed and then stopped. His heart gave three more beats and stopped, followed by a final shallow exhale. Clarence was gone.

JOHN . . .

John could be very manipulative. He had much of the nursing staff upset with him and was burning out most of his friends. He would refuse medication and food. He went through depressions where he refused to care for himself at all—he would insist that people help him. He had running battles with the staff, the courts, various members of his family, and, at times, with me.

This made for a challenging hospice relationship. One day, when the nursing staff was trying to wean him from a wheelchair he didn't need, I refused to wheel him down to the day room on his ward. He threatened to fire me as his hospice volunteer. I firmly told him that he needed to walk. He jumped up and threw his wheelchair at me, then stormed off to the day room. That evening

I heard that I had been fired (for the third or fourth time). I stayed away for a few days. When I returned, all John said was, "Where have you been?"

It was frustrating not knowing whether to help John or to encourage him to do things for himself. I was his hospice volunteer for fourteen months, and would spend time with him daily. On weekends we would often spend all afternoon together, especially when I could convince him to go out into the yard in nice weather. At one point, frustrated that the courts would not grant him an early medical release, John quit eating. He was determined to either get sick enough that they would let him go home, or just die and get it over with. He became so weak that he was transferred to an acute care ward.

One Friday morning, I went to take him down to the Jewish service. He could still dress himself, but as he often did, he just laid there looking at me, waiting for me to dress him, daring me to complain. We were going to be late, and I didn't feel up to the struggle. I reached for his socks and started putting them on his feet. I used to do this too, as an attendant for my teacher Chögyam Trungpa Rinpoche, who was partially paralyzed. As I tried to put on one of John's socks without hurting him, I had a sudden flash of my teacher lying there before me. For a moment, John transformed into my teacher, and I felt a wave of devotion and longing overcome me. From that moment, I never felt the slightest hesitation or doubt in caring for John. The whole issue of manipulation and enabling fell away for me.

John eventually received the early medical release he so desired, and died peacefully—a free man—with an old friend by his side, in a Miami hospital two days after leaving prison.

Hospice work took me down many paths. I worked with men from a whole spectrum of social and religious backgrounds: smugglers, swindlers, bikers, bank robbers and bankers: Americans, Cubans, Mexicans, Colombians, Native Americans and Haitians—Catholics, Protestants and atheists—dozens of patients in all. Many of them I became very close to and will never forget, but one of the most memorable was my Native American friend, Joe Star.

JOE . . .

"We're going to cook you good today, Bro. This is going to be a real warrior's sweat," said my friend Joe as I wheeled him up the ramp toward the chapel area.

"Oh, great," I thought to myself, knowing that I had a hard enough time with the heat anyway. I'd been in the sweat lodge many times in my years in prison, and sometimes I felt like I was about to succumb to heat stroke.

Fortunately, it wasn't too hot that day, so we would get a little relief whenever the lodge door was opened. I wheeled Joe through the chapel out to the open area where the lodge was situated. Several of the lodge brothers were already there building the fire to heat the rocks. Joe was grinning widely at the thought of the intense sweat he had planned for me, his little Bro.

73

I was a little frightened, even though I normally look forward to being in the sweat lodge. It is a powerful spiritual and healing practice, and afterward I always felt renewed, awake, and reconnected to my essential being. The extreme heat scares me, though, especially when the brothers get macho about it, and it looked like today was going to be one of those days.

Joe had been battling lung cancer for about a year. He'd been through rough times with cycles of radiation and chemotherapy. Yet, he saw the whole experience as a warrior's challenge and would describe it to me in terms reminiscent of a traditional shaman's journey into death. We had been working together for some time, using two books, *The Way of the Pipe* by John Redtail, and *Healing Into Life and Death* by Stephen Levine, as the basis for our discussions and meditations.

Joe respected my Buddhist training and practice experience, but this sweat was to be my test: he was still checking me out to see if real warrior's blood ran in my veins or not.

The heat was so intense and suffocating during the first round that I was on the edge of losing consciousness. As I was gasping for air though, I suddenly remembered to slow down my breathing. I slowly sucked the scorching air deep into my lungs, and the heat sent me into a sort of trance for the rest of the round. The heat, the drumming, the singing, and the prayers, all combined amidst a background of fear, the fear of dying.

The second round was worse than the first. I don't know how long it lasted, but I was just about to yell, "*Ho Mitakuye Oyasin*" (All My Relations) the Lakota prayer that also serves as the request for the door to be opened, when the sweat leader himself, to my relief, called it out. We all chimed in with the most resounding *Ho Mitakuye Oyasin* I'd ever heard in the lodge. I couldn't have lasted another minute. After two more rounds, each more intense, I finally collapsed on the ground and lay there a long time.

While wheeling Joe back through the chapel, the chaplain stopped us and asked Joe, "What did you do to Fleet? He's red as a lobster." Joe just smiled and said, "Yeah, that was a good one, a real warrior's sweat. You made it, Bro. You're a warrior now."

That was little consolation at the time. I felt like I might get sick, and Joe looked pretty done in, too; he just slumped down in his wheelchair for the rest of the trip back, and neither one of us spoke.

Joe died of lung cancer about two months later. Two days before his death, we had one last time together in the sacred sweat lodge, in the elements where Joe was completely at home. This was a gentler sweat; Joe was preparing to die. He remained in the lodge after the Inipi (*sweat lodge*) ceremony, including the final passing of the sacred pipe, had concluded.

Even as we removed the blankets from the willow saplings that form the lodge, Joe lay there on the ground, close to the still warm rocks, curled up in a fetal position, face down on his beloved grandmother Earth. One of the lodge brothers became concerned, thinking maybe Joe had died. I whispered, "No, I don't think so, but I think he's practicing."

Joe had talked to me many times about his long walks in the mountains near his home, and of the many things he had learned about the plants and animals there. He liked to tell me how when animals got sick, they would curl up in a secluded place and wait until they healed up or died. Joe often said that he would do the same if he could go home, so I wasn't surprised when he elected to die alone.

I never saw him alive again after that last sweat. Two days after the sweat, I was called to the ward and got there about twenty minutes after he had died. I sat with Joe's body, said prayers, and told him good-bye. I wished I had known one of the lodge songs well enough to sing for him then. But I guess we had already sung our last song together.

At that moment, I could almost smell the fire and hear the drum and the songs. I was happy to know that Joe was finally on his way home, where his family had been preparing special ceremonial clothing for his burial. I hoped Joe's spirit would be able to pay one last visit to his beloved New Mexico mountains before moving on to his next journey. I wished I had been there for him, though I knew it was his choice to be alone.

Finally, the guards came in to photograph his body and pack his things. I tried to conceal my tears as I passed them on the way out. I felt happy and sad, exposed and raw, but good, alive and human. This moment was a precious gift in this prison world, a world that conspires to close your heart and rob you of your humanity—this moment of tender sadness was a gift from my friend Joe.

Chapter 5
LETTING GO OF DEPRESSION

The specter of depression accompanied me in my prison experience from the very beginning. It was always there, just over my shoulder, at the edge of my consciousness, a black hole of despair and darkness. There were times in the county jail, awaiting trial and then sentencing, that I just wanted to lie down and die. The moment I received a thirty-year no-parole sentence, my knees buckled. My lawyer had to hold me up. It was surreal. I could hear the prosecution celebrating, just as they'd done when the jury returned a guilty verdict on all counts. I experienced my life ending right there on the spot. The reality of losing my son, my family, and my entire life as I knew it, hit me with a pain and devastation I'd never known. My mind was spinning. I could barely focus on my surroundings. The only thought I could hold onto was, "Don't let the bastards see you cry."

I had witnessed the U.S. Marshals making fun of prisoners'

reactions to their sentencing while sitting in the holding cell at the courthouse during breaks in my trial. I had promised myself I wouldn't give them the pleasure of seeing me break down. Somehow, I violently stuffed down the pain at that moment. Later that night, alone in my cell when I desperately wanted to cry, I couldn't. They put me in an isolation cell in an otherwise empty wing of a county jail with a camera on me. I assumed I was under suicide watch. It was a long, dark, mostly sleepless night, sitting at the edge of an abyss. At the darkest moment, something rose up in me, and I made a decision to live and to survive. The darkness remained with me though, always inviting me—as if the possibility of giving up would be an escape from my pain.

In prison, there's an edge of depression that you deal with all the time, especially when you have a long sentence. The time felt endless. Sometimes, I felt I'd been in prison for so long I couldn't see the end. There was no light at the end of the tunnel, and I didn't know if I would get out of there alive. In our hospice program, I worked with men all the time who were my age and younger, who came down with cancer and never got out—dying alone in prison. I also thought about the violence. If you kept your head down, you could avoid most of it, but you just never knew.

Ultimately, my years in prison became a powerfully transformative and deeply liberating experience for me. But inside, the pain of pain, loss and hopelessness still arose frequently. Most of the time I managed not to dwell on the fact of my time, the years, months and days I had left; or it would have driven me nuts. Sometimes it was just unavoidable though, and I would just find myself staring my sentence of twenty-five years (reduced from 30 upon appeal some three years into my prison journey) straight in the face with nothing to take away the pain. I'd see and feel the reality of never going home. I'd think of my son growing up without his dad. It would bring me to the most acute edge of pain, beyond what I imagined I could bear. I'd find myself at the point of screaming, or beating my head on the concrete wall of my cell, or just collapsing into a black hole of despair and darkness.

After years of training my mind through daily meditation and intensive retreat practice in prison, my experience of this pain and darkness began to shift dramatically. I would find myself in the midst of this intense hopelessness and pain, burning with an agony that was almost blinding, and my awareness or practice mind would somehow just hold the experience—meaning I would just stay with the direct experience without going into a lot of thoughts about it. When this happened, I then experienced that awareness as a spaciousness growing around the intense pain. Then the pain would dissolve into space, leaving me in a state of joy, almost a kind of bliss. This was a bizarre and unsettling experience the first time it happened; but with time, I came to accept it and appreciate that my meditation practice had given me a way to work with and transform my pain and dispair.

The experience of letting go, of seeing and feeling the pain acutely, and then experiencing it dissolve into spaciousness and joy was the supreme gift. It gave me a profound confidence about life, my spiritual path and meditation practice, and the workability of any situation, no matter how frightening or painful.

These transformative experiences arising from my meditation practice in the midst of the pain and despair of long-term incarceration led to an overall experience of basic cheerfulness that wasn't based on anything. In ordinary terms, there was absolutely no reason to be cheerful in prison. There was nothing in my environment or daily life at that point to be particularly happy about—quite the contrary. My life was a disaster by any conventional measure. Nonetheless, at that edge of depression, I found a joy that was not based on anything going on outside, leading to an unshakeable confidence in something good and trustworthy at the core of my being. My own direct experience of this transformation of pain and depression into joy and cheerfulness is one of the main reasons why I believe deeply in the power of meditation to change our prisons from the inside out.

In hospice work, depression could be a real enemy. One of my first patients was a cantankerous former biker and entertainer named John. When I was first introduced to John as his hospice volunteer, two things had just happened. First, John's early medical release had been revoked, literally as he was on his way down to "R&D" to be processed for release. Evidently the nursing staff and doctors had informed the parole board that John was responding to his cancer treatment, so the board decided to revoke his early medical parole (a type of release occasionally granted to prisoners so they can die at home with family) at the last minute. Almost immediately following that, John got word that his father died. They were extremely close, and John was distraught. He had given up, and his appearance showed it. He hadn't bathed in weeks. His long hair and beard were dirty and disheveled and his finger nails needed trimming and cleaning badly. His hospital room was a mess. I was surprised that the prison staff had allowed things to reach this point.

Over the ensuing weeks, I managed to get John to clean up a bit, go out the yard on nice days, and generally reengage with life. As his depression lifted, it was replaced with anger and a fierce determination to get out of prison at all costs. John began pursuing every legal remedy possible and started writing to every outside organization that could possibly support his campaign to reclaim his lost medical parole. He was determined not to die in prison. Over the next year, John went up and down many times, vacillating between hope and fear, between anger and depression. At one point, he gave up on his legal and letter writing campaign and decided to just let himself get so sick that they would either release him or he would die and be done with it. He stopped eating and quickly began to decline. In the end, they finally did release him with an early medical parole. He died two days later in an outside hospital, accompanied by an old friend, having achieved a victory of sorts within the perverse context of our criminal justice system.

Over the years, among the many medical and psychiatric patients I worked with in the prison hospice program, in the school where I taught GED classes, and through the meditation group I lead in the prison chapel, I saw a lot of men give up, letting themselves slide into hopelessness, depression and sometimes death. I even saw this in some of the general population inmates like myself, who would find their way into the hole or even the psychiatric ward, no longer able to find a reason to hang in there with their prison time having lost their vision for a life and a future beyond the walls.

To say I'm grateful that not only did I not succumb to this kind of despair but that I found a way through meditation to work with depression and transform it to cheerfulness and even joy, is an understatement of immense proportions. My hope is that along the way, this potential for transformation may have rubbed off on a few of my fellow prisoners.

Chapter 6
RUMBLINGS FROM THE INSIDE

Taken from material originally published in Tikkun *magazine,* *March/April 1998.*

The other day at mail call, which follows the 4pm "standing, bedside count," I received a kind letter from Ms. Carol Evans, a social worker at an inner city New Orleans hospice. Carol thanked me for the prison hospice literature and training materials I'd sent her to help her organization establish an inmate-staffed prison hospice program at the Louisiana State Penitentiary in Angola. This hospice program now serves the many lifers who die at this infamous maximum security prison.

It's difficult for me to express the deep gratitude and satisfaction I felt in reading Ms. Evans' letter. Daily prison life consists of experiences of quite the opposite sort. Instead of kindness and appreciation, the prison environment communicates—day in and day out—something very different to prisoners—shame.

As we go about our day, shame is built into the wake-ups, the body counts, the prison jobs, the mainline stampedes to the mess hall, the body searches upon leaving the mess hall, the periodic room shakedowns and urine drops for drug testing, and the "bend them over and spread'em" full body searches coming and going from the visiting room.

There are continual shaming messages built into the system, consciously and unconsciously reinforced by staff and prisoners alike, reminding us that we are second class human beings at best—just bodies to count, and of no real value other than as grist for the mill of the growing corrections industry. Even when staff and prisoners exchange pleasantries or good-natured banter, the subtle or not so subtle message is almost always there: "You're an inmate, a thug, a criminal—I'm not. I am a human being. I count—you don't."

I'm often amazed at how well prisoners seem to get along in such a negative and disheartening atmosphere. But we pay a great price for such excellent adaptation. We steel ourselves with layers and layers of anger and bitterness, shielding ourselves from the external barrage of condemnation and the internal world of vulnerability and pain—the fear and loneliness in our gut. We are buried under a mountain of guilt, shame, and demonization heaped upon us by prosecutors, judges, jailors, the media, politicians, correctional staff, and society. This makes it very difficult to feel the genuine remorse and regret necessary for change and healing. Instead we tend to project our shame and self-hatred outward in the form of anger, bitterness, and hostility toward the system and its representatives—the prison staff and the police.

Most of us don't walk around with grim faces all day. There's actually a lot of humor here, albeit dark humor for the most part. But just scratch the surface with almost any prisoner, and you will find raw anger and bitterness, even explosive rage. Just ask the right question, and most of us will launch into our story—a well-rehearsed monologue describing in detail how bad we've been abused and maligned by the government, prosecutors and judges, our attorneys, our former crime partners turned informants, and eventually by our wives or girlfriends. Such relationships tend to unravel within a few months or a year at best. It's a rare prisoner who acknowledges any part he or she might have had in all this chaos and pain. Our stories are instead all about anger, blame, justification, and resentment. It's all about Them—never Us.

Some of us eventually tire of hearing ourselves telling this same bitter story over and over again. We also tire of hearing our fellow prisoners' stories and become skilled at avoiding them. I became thoroughly bored with my own story many years ago, and I am always quite chagrined when some chance encounter with another prisoner's story gets me going, even momentarily, on mine again. I admit to avoiding newcomers and their stories like the plague; but when I do stumble into one, I try to listen with compassion, remembering my deep need to vent anger and frustration with someone after my own trial and sentencing.

Bo Lozoff, the author of *We're All Doing Time* and founder of the Human Kindness Foundation, explains that the problem with our past and current approaches to penology—namely the rehabilitation and punishment models—is that they both make the prisoner the sole focus of attention, thus reinforcing the already strong narcissistic character traits which brought most of us to prison in the first place. Those favoring rehabilitation have primarily pushed the treatment model, making the prisoner the focal point of various psychodynamic, cognitive, and behavior modification treatment strategies, in effect turning prisoners into clients or patients. The punishment model does essentially the same thing, except in this case the treatment combines callous, lock-em-up warehousing with continual reinforcement of prisoners' self-hatred: "You're no good, you're a criminal, an animal, a thug," which leads to: "I'm no good, I'm a criminal, I'm an animal, a thug."

Neither approach encourages, much less empowers, prisoners to take responsibility for what they've done, to make amends, or to change themselves and their future. The current system demands that prisoners be docile, institutionalized consumers of penology, whatever form that takes. The most recent trend is to turn prisoners into low-wage workers for prison industries and consumers of prison commissary stores and lucrative telephone contract services, creating wealth for companies well-placed in the newly emerging prison industrial complex.

In prison, we get used to people doing things for us—making decisions for us, providing programs, meals, medical services, laundry. This can encourage us to fall into a dependent and consumerist mentality. Of course, the same thing happens on the outside, as witnessed by our consumerism-dominated world.

This punishment model will only produce waves of angry, bitter, desperate, broken men and women coming out of prison year after year. The currently out-of-fashion treatment model tends to produce dependent, narcissistic ex-cons who feel they should continue to be centers of attention upon release, treating their families and communities as if they were somehow owed a lifetime of special treatment and support.

Lozoff suggests that we instead take the radical approach of treating prisoners with kindness, decency and respect while empowering them to take responsibility for changing their own lives through work, education and service. He encourages us to find avenues of service, volunteer activities responding to needs inside and outside prison, as a way of getting out of ourselves and our stories and focusing instead on the needs of others.

Prison hospice programs are one such avenue. With hospice care patients don't die a lonely, bleak death devoid of the caring presence of another human being. Hundreds of prison hospice of volunteers and patients alike have had the opportunity to move beyond resentment, blame, and justification game, and deal with the issues of their lives and the consequences of their pasts. Death has become the great teacher, guiding us to discover the basic goodness inherent in ourselves and others and the compassion which flows naturally from an open heart.

Following the path of meditation in prison is another avenue for taking responsibility and accountability for our lives. It can also offer a way to be of service to our fellow prisoners. It isn't always easy to find support, resources and materials in prison to help one begin a meditation practice or contemplative spiritual path. We often have trouble getting books, liturgies, meditation instruction and supplies. Many prisoners still have little or no access to outside dharma teachers and guides. So, what are we to do? Wait for someone on the outside to get it together and bring a dharma program to our prison? With that approach, we could wait a long time. Instead, we could cultivate our own resources and work with what we have. I don't believe the meditation groups that flourish inside will be established only by outside volunteers. I believe that the ultimate success and cultivation of any prison or jail mediation program will have a lot to do with us—the men and women behind bars, thirsting for truth and a path to true freedom.

Many of us inside are consumers, taking advantage of things provided by others. We've been conditioned this way our whole lives. Despite this conditioning, the programs in prisons— recovery meetings, chapel groups, educational and athletic programs—are sometimes created and coordinated by prisoners themselves. They show up every week, setting up the space, creating a beneficial situation for others and serving their community. In some cases, it is the prison staff or outside volunteers who create programs. But, in other cases, prisoners are carrying the load, being the source for the programs which create opportunities for change in our prison world.

I encourage all prisoners who have made a connection with meditation to become the person, or part of the core group, who establishes meditation practice as an available spiritual path at their institutions. You don't have to have experience to set up a group. By contacting outside support organizations like Prison Dharma Network (PDN), you can acquire basic Dharma books from Tibetan, Zen, Vipassana and other traditions, as well as meditation instructions and basic guidelines for setting up a group. Anyone can organize a study group or simply gather with like-minded fellow prisoners to study and practice together. This doesn't mean setting yourself up as a leader, teacher, or any kind of authority, but rather as a fellow practitioner in service of others.

Some of us have encountered negative attitudes or ignorance in relation to our prison chaplains. I encourage prisoners not to be discouraged by this or to allow themselves to be drawn into confrontations which will not serve anyone.

In working to establish the Dharma in prison settings, I feel it is essential to model the teachings we hope to learn and make available to others—principles like gentleness, equanimity, and compassion. With patience, friendliness, and good humor we can gradually educate staff about the benefits of meditation. When they see good qualities manifesting in our behavior, even in the face of resistance, they will be impressed and gradually become more open to the transformational quality of these practices.

While incarcerated, I sourced a prison dharma group in a federal prison for over thirteen years. Twice a week I arrived at the chapel early to set up an altar and put out the meditation cushions. I worked with the chaplains to assure that we had a space and time to meet and resources like meditation cushions for practice, and books and videos for study.

In all those years, there were only a handful of prisoners who joined me in directly supporting the group. Hundreds more just came, made use of what we had to offer, and went on their way. Hopefully, the seeds of practice later flourished in many of these men. In my experience though, it was those few men who genuinely got involved in supporting the group that really connected most deeply with the path of Dharma. Several went on to establish groups at other prisons, and most of them are now committed practitioners and contributing members of outside *sanghas* (Buddhist communities). If any prisoner is genuinely interested in the path of meditation, I would strongly encourage them to move beyond the consumer mindset and find

91

a way to be a source for establishing meditation programs in your institution. In doing so, you will benefit many and surely encounter the true Dharma yourself. You will rise above the level of shame-based dehumanization and become a living example of the truth that practicing dharma can alleviate suffering.

Chapter 7
A TASTE OF FREEDOM

From the Shambhala Sun

After more than thirteen years behind bars, a prisoner's short, bittersweet experience of freedom is a reminder of his guru and the free, cheerful state of mind that is available at every moment.

The guard inside the control center motioned me closer to the glass to I.D. me, and suddenly the outer glass windows of the sally port slid open. I stepped out into the free world, relishing each moment with amazement as I walked down the stone steps of the main entrance to the maximum-security federal prison hospital in Springfield, Missouri. The day was absolutely beautiful, not a cloud in the brilliant azure sky. The autumn air was just a little crisp but the afternoon sun bathed me in its warmth. A huge U.S. flag beat smartly in the breeze, high atop its flagpole just across from the main entrance guard tower.

Just short of thirteen years ago, I had arrived at this prison in handcuffs and leg irons, wearing a bright orange, county jail jumpsuit. Now, I was in the free world again, wearing slacks, a sports coat and tie, waiting for a taxi to the airport. After being locked up continuously for thirteen and a half years (including seven months in a county jail), I couldn't believe I was standing there on my own—no handcuffs, no guards, no fear. It was time for the afternoon shift change, and quite a few staff were coming and going. Some who knew me waved; a few stopped to chat. The rest simply paid me no mind at all. Just minutes earlier I had been an inmate inside a high security prison, where the slightest challenge to authority was met with swift and sure suppression. Now, just because of where I was standing and the clothes I was wearing, I was suddenly seen as a normal human being.

Standing there at the curb, I had a jumble of intense feelings. My father had died just the day before. I was headed home on a three-day unescorted furlough to attend the funeral and be with my family. My dad had fought lung cancer valiantly during the past seven months. He'd had thirty one radiation treatments and four rounds of chemotherapy and seemed to be winning, but a few weeks short of his 78th birthday, his damaged lungs and embattled heart finally gave out.

My greatest fear, losing one of my parents while still locked up, had come to pass. My greatest hope, that my dad would survive to see me walk out of prison for good, was not to be. The day before, when I found out over the phone that my dad had died,

I went back to my cell and fell apart. I cried and cried. Now I was standing out in the fresh air and sunshine, hurting like hell inside and grinning on the outside at the beauty and majesty of a fall afternoon in the Ozarks.

Unescorted funeral furloughs are all but unheard of at this maximum-security prison. The standard practice is to send the prisoner in handcuffs and leg irons with an escort of two guards, sometimes four. You are only allowed to attend the actual funeral ceremony and burial, and you pay all the expenses, including overtime for the guards. I had really dreaded showing up at my dad's funeral escorted by prison guards. As a low security prisoner only six months short of release to a halfway house, I'd long been eligible for transfer to a minimum security prison camp, and the only reason I remained in the high security institution was to continue the hospice work I'd been doing here since 1987. Even so, the warden was sticking his neck out by letting me go, and I was very grateful for his compassionate decision.

Standing, gazing into the sky, I couldn't help but think of my Buddhist teacher, Chogyam Trungpa Rinpoche. To this day, whenever I look at the sky, especially a deep blue cloudless sky, I am reminded of my teacher and the joy I always felt in his presence. I had been in prison almost two years when he died in 1987. I was devastated by my teacher's death and overwhelmed by deep regrets. I felt I had let him down in so many ways. He was my best friend and had given me everything, but at the end of his life, I wasn't even there.

During the weeks following his death, I spent a lot of time walking the track in the prison yard. There, his presence was especially potent for me, somehow embodied in the vastness of the sky. Although I expected to be thoroughly depressed, I actually awoke each morning in a very cheerful state, and this uplifted state of mind remained unshakable throughout the day, sometimes approaching a state of elation or mild rapture, especially outside, when I was walking the prison yard. Of course, I experienced a powerful sense of emptiness and impermanence as the death of my teacher began to sink in, but these feelings were like ripples in a more powerful and very stable positive state of mind.

Thinking about my dad and gazing at the clear blue sky, I recognized that raw, tenderhearted mixture of joy and sadness Trungpa Rinpoche described as the mark of being truly awake and alive. One of his most important teachings was that we could simply cheer up by connecting with our inherent sanity and healthiness, what he called Basic Goodness. Rinpoche taught that there is an unlimited source of cheerful, awake energy always available to us. Because I was rather thick-headed, it took getting locked up in prison for me to start practicing enough to realize the truth of this teaching. After years of daily practice and yearly retreats, that unconditional, cheerful mind became the context of my daily life in prison, immediately available even if not always present. To say I'm grateful for this would be no small understatement.

The three days I spent at home with my family were a great blessing, even in the circumstance of such loss and sadness. It was hard to grasp being out in the free world again. Everything had a surreal quality to it, especially on the day of the funeral. I couldn't even imagine what it was like for the rest of my family. They had been through all this just four months earlier with the tragic death of my 17-year-old nephew, David—same funeral home, same church, same cemetery. Just short of starting his senior year in high school, this free-spirited and much-loved young man fell to his death while attempting to climb down some river bluffs at night with his buddies. My dad was deeply grieved over the senseless death of his grandson, and now we were going to bury him too.

I wanted to take my dad's body back to the house and just hang out with him for a while, at least a few days or a week, like people did in the old days. Now everything is so fast, so busy. I needed more time with my dad, more time to cry and laugh and grieve for him. The ride to the cemetery was really hard. My mom, who had been very strong and steady up until then, began to have a very difficult time. She said, "I just can't believe we are really doing this—really going to bury your father." I spent most of my three days at home at my mother's side. It meant everything to me, and I know it meant the world to her to have me there.

It was strange to return to the prison in a taxi and ask someone to let me in. Furloughs are so rare at this prison that the guards outside didn't quite know what to do with me. The guard who eventually let me into the prisoner receiving area said, "Welcome back," the irony immediately obvious to both of us. It took me just a few minutes to be strip-searched ("Bend over and spread 'em") and forced to change from my street clothes back into prison khakis. Dressed again in inmate attire, I was amazed how quickly the attitude of the guards shifted. The usual arrogant attitude and sick, "We've got your ass" prison guard humor started up immediately. Well, at least I knew I was "home."

Despite being busy with numerous projects and my usual intense daily schedule, I've been in a deeply reflective mood since returning to the prison, carried along by a river of complex and unpredictable emotions. Anger and sadness, fear and loneliness, emptiness and longing have colored my days and nights, interspersed with feelings of peace and even joy at moments of acceptance and letting go. It all comes and goes of its own accord.

Nothing prepared me for losing one of my parents—not the hospice work I've been doing here for the past eleven years, not the meditation practices I've been doing for more than twenty years, not even the death of my own spiritual teacher. My father had always been a powerful reference point in my life , a presence I battled with at times. In recent years we had grown very close and talked regularly by phone. The final time had been just days before he entered the hospital for the last time. I knew I loved my dad a lot and told him so regularly. But only when I saw his lifeless body laid out in a casket at the funeral home did I fully realize how deeply I loved him. It broke my heart.

I have let a lot of people down in my life—my mom and dad, my teacher, my son, and many others. Somehow everyone has stuck with me. I have been the beneficiary of so much kindness from so many people. It amazes me and it inspires me to want to do something of value with my life, to be of service in some way.

I have been studying with Roshi Bernie Glassman for the past five years, inspired by his unique approach to contemplative social action. I would like to work with others when I get out to establish a peacemaker village centered around prison ministry and prison reform activism. I have lived in this prison world long enough that it's now part of who I am. I could never just walk away from it.

As Buddhists, we aspire to experience all beings as family; I know all prisoners are my sisters and brothers. The prison situation in the U.S. is getting worse and the challenge is immense—to slow down current trends, bring about reforms, and minister to the needs of the millions of men, women and children living with the realities of the system. It looks like there's an almost unlimited future in prison activism. It's nice to have a mission in life, but it's a job I would very much like to work myself out of.

262330

Chapter 8
TRANSFORMING OBSTACLES INTO PATH

from a talk Fleet gave two weeks after his release.
Boulder Shambhala Center, June 1999

As a Buddhist practitioner who ended up in prison for 14 years—it somewhat begs the question, "How did that happen?" You don't run into too many experienced meditation practitioners in prison!

My life, growing up in the 60s, became a pursuit of looking for something genuine or real. This pursuit was based on memories of early childhood when life seemed to me to be magical. I had clear memories of that magical time and also clear memories of when it went away. The natural loss of innocence that happens to us all at a young age, called "growing up"—I'd never quite come to terms with. I yearned for the feeling that I was really connected and open to the world. This longing pulled me into a spiritual search and left me disillusioned with the social and religious world in which I was raised.

This yearning also led me into using drugs and alcohol. I graduated from high school angry and disillusioned. I arrived at a large midwestern university in the fall of 1968, and jumped headlong into the counterculture, drug culture and radical politics of the day. Eventually, I developed an "outlaw" mentality—wanting to live outside the system. I had a solid "us" and "them" attitude— seeing the current socio/political system as corrupt and hypocritical and imagining myself as a member of an alternative culture grounded in peace and love. I left college behind in 1972 and moved to South America to live as a hippie, outlaw, spiritual seeker, and expatriate. There I pursued various spiritual paths, tried to learn to meditate, and specifically studied Buddhism. Of course, I was still involved with drug use.

In order to continue my expatriate, counterculture lifestyle, I seized upon opportunities that led me to smuggling drugs as a part-time job. At that time I was living in a house high in the Andes mountains, above the village of Urubamba in the the Sacred Valley of the Incas, near Cusco, Peru. In order to get to where I lived you had to hitch a ride on a truck for a couple of hours and hike a long trail heading up to one of the glaciers above the sacred valley.

In 1974, a traveler hiked up to our house. He brought a copy of *Rolling Stone* magazine which had an article about the first summer session of the Naropa Institute (now Naropa University). Reading the article I just *knew* I had to go to Naropa. Soon thereafter, I decided to visit Boulder, Colorado where Naropa is located. After this visit I decided to move back to the U.S. and get a degree in Contemplative Psychotherapy from Naropa. In the meantime, I had married a young woman from Cusco, who was now pregnant with our child. So I packed up my family and moved to Boulder so that I could begin my studies. It was here that I connected with my teacher Chogyam Trungpa Rinpoche. After arriving at Naropa, I got very involved in practice and attended many long meditation programs and retreats. I also had the opportunity to be in Rinpoche's service and spend a lot of time with him. Unfortunately at the same time, I was still abusing alcohol and drugs and still dabbling in my part-time profession as a drug smuggler.

I was receiving a tremendous amount of training and teachings from my Buddhist community and teachers, but at the same time I was maintaining a secret life of drug smuggler, addict and crazy person. In the Buddhist world, I didn't let too much of my drug world craziness leak out. But when I went off into my secret world—it was wild. With all this craziness, I never really developed a disciplined daily meditation practice outside of programs and retreats. Inside, I knew I *had* to get out of the drug world—but I was hooked and couldn't manage to leave it behind.

Then my world all fell apart. My marriage was in chaos, my addictions were out of control and now—on top of all that—I was being investigated by federal agents. The gig was up. I was finally forced to give up my criminal career. For a year and a half before going to prison, I worked as a car salesman and survived like an "ordinary" person, supporting my family. At the same time, I knew I was facing anywhere from 20 years to life in prison with no-parole. The agents were promising my lawyer they'd put me away for at least 30 years. Needless to say, I was experiencing extremes of anxiety. Throughout this time, I continued to medicate myself with alcohol as a way to alleviate my fears.

I faced the choice of taking off and running from the law, or staying and facing my situation. It's fortunate I didn't have a lot of money then. If I'd had money, I would have been much more tempted to take off. The idea of being on the run, with or without money, didn't hold much appeal—but the idea of going to prison for 30 years terrified me.

I sought counsel with senior teachers in my Buddhist community, and they advised me to stick around and work with the situation I'd created for myself, bringing it to the path of practice. On the run, it would be impossibe to maintain the connection with my teacher, Trungpa Rinpoche, and with my community and family.

I was indicted in May 1985. One day I was here in Boulder and the next I flew to St. Louis to turn myself in. That was it—I never got out again.

Probably the toughest time of my prison journey was the first seven months I spent in the county jail. County jails can be hellish—they are usually worse than prison. There *are* some very hellish prisons—but most jails are worse. I was experiencing extreme levels of stress at that point. The government was spending nearly half a million dollars to bury me. It's quite an experience—the United States Government versus you—no contest from the get go. What I had done to my family was horrible. My family are prominent people in St. Louis and due to weird circumstances, which were completely my fault, and the governments desire for publicity, my trial ended up in their home town. Because of my mistakes, my family had to undergo the shame of a huge front page scandal—one of my most painful regrets.

My son and wife were left penniless without a father, husband or provider. On top of that, I'd thrown a number of close friends into some sticky situations of being investigated by the authorities.

I had created a tremendous mess. I was living with that mess and my life was in utter chaos. I couldn't sleep, my mind raced constantly with agony, guilt, shame, remorse and fantasies of escape. I shared a tiny cell with a toilet and sink that often didn't work. It was a very intimate living situation, and you didn't want to go to the bathroom with your bunkie (cell mate) in the cell, he wouldn't want to be there—so you had to work all these things out. The possibility of conflict and violence was in your face all the time.

We lived with constant noise, television and radios blaring 24 hours a day, prisoners screaming back and forth between cell blocks and fights erupting all the time, especially the cell blocks holding the local county and state prisoners in that southern Missouri jail. Every now and then they would bring someone over to our cell block, reserved for federal prisoners awaiting trial in St. Louis, who was beaten up in one of the other blocks and have us take care of him. Even in our block, there was constant noise and chaos and guys that stayed up all night talking. I was barely sleeping and my mind was in chaos. I knew at that point that I had to start practicing. I'd at least learned that much from my days in Boulder in the Buddhist community. So I got to where I was practicing sitting meditation four to five hours a day while waiting for trial.

One day I'd been sitting on the upper bunk in my cell for five hours trying my best to work with my mind in meditation. People were yelling and screaming and all the usual chaos was happening, but I suddenly noticed that my mind wasn't moving. My mind wasn't being pulled or distracted by all the noise. I was completely aware of the chaos and noise, but my mind wasn't moving like it normally would, drifting into all kinds of thoughts about my reactions to the chaos—thoughts of irritation or annoyance or even thoughts of trying to block it out. Instead I felt calm and peaceful, just resting in a steady and seemingly indestructable awareness of the present moment. That was an amazing experience, given the situation. I had experienced similar states in various meditation retreats before coming to prison, where my mind just rested with 'what is,'—but never in the midst of such chaos. This was a pivotal experience that told me that whatever I was going to go through on this prison journey was workable if I just trained in calming my own mind and stablizing meditative awareness under any circumstances.

And I knew that the only way for me to calm my mind, and tame my reactive thoughts was to dedicate myself to the daily practice of sitting meditation. So, I carried this realization with me when I was transfered to the federal prison system after sentencing. The institution in Springfield, Missouri where I was sent, was a maximum-security, federal prison hospital with 1000 medical and psychiatric patients and about 300 general populations inmates like myself, who were sent there to work in food service, housekeeping, maintenance, etc. I was actually fortunate to be sent there. Due to the lenght of my sentence, I was almost certain that I would be going to the nearest federal penitentiary, USP Leavenworth, one of the toughest maximum security prisons in the country, located in Leavenworth, Kansas.

When I arrived at my new "home," MCFP Springfield, I was still very much caught up in the drama of my own situation. Many thoughts were going through my mind about the hopelessness of my situation, and my thirty-year, no-parole sentence (later reduced to 25 years on appeal), as I walked in the door of the prison. I was almost immediately struck by the immensity of suffering there, by all the people suffering and dying there. I saw people in wheelchairs, paraplegics and quadraplegics, people in tremendous pain, emaciated, dying of AIDS and other illness, men obviously heavily medicated with psychotropic drugs, even blind men feeling their way down a dark prison corridor. I was vividly aware, seeing these men suffer so, that they had it much worse than I did. It shook me out of my personal drama and anxious thoughts immediately.

I soon set about getting involved in my new world. I knew as I entered this world that I could choose one of two forks in the road—I could either be a hermit, doing a lot of practice, removed from it all, or, I could make this place my life and get really involved and make a difference trying to help with all the suffering there. It was pretty obvious that the latter was the only choice for me. The example set by my spiritual teacher Trungpa Rinpoche would hardly let me do otherwise. At the same time, I knew that anything that would happen with regard to offering meditation training or helping with the patients in some way, would grow not out of manipulating or strategizing or being a well meaning 'do gooder'—but rather out of the foundation of my own meditation practice. Meditation practice gives me the ability to "get myself out of the way"—meaning, to get my personal drama and complaints out of the way so that I could serve the greater good.

So, I started practicing a lot and also figured out ways to be of service. I started a meditation group. I got involved in showing movies to dying patients. I became very concerned with the AIDS situation. At this hospital, the AIDS patients were locked away from the general population for their own security. There was a lot of fear in 1985 about AIDS. I started writing to AIDS advocacy organizations on the outside and other death and dying experts. This eventually led to the formation of an inmate staffed hospice program in the prison.

In prison I had to make a choice to really *live* there, not in my fantasies of what might've been, and to try to really practice what I had received on the outside from my Buddhist teachers. People have told me that they are amazed or inspired by that. But actually I had no choice. My connection with my teacher Chogyam Trungpa was always there—it was as if he was right there at my shoulder—so what else could I do but try to practice what I'd been taught? I was very fortunate, because most people don't come into prison with the kind of tools and resources I had. So I was relentless in my practice. Often, I would get up at 3am and practice. This created a powerful momentum for the work I was doing with the mediation group and the hospice work. And it also created interest from other prisoners, and from that, groups of practitioners grew.

Prison, on a lot of levels, is a really flaky world, but at the same time people inside demand each other to be *real*. Some prisoners play at being real and try to get respect for their act or racket, but when that happens, it's basically bullshit. But when somebody can be real, and by that I mean being truly authentic, honest, present, and connected with the power of who you are, it creates a lot of power and generates respect. Although sometimes it can generate resentment and backlash as well. But I found that generally if I was true and honest with myself about who I was as well as who I wasn't, and if I was kind and respectful of others, they responded in kind.

So, the title of this talk tonight is "Transforming Obstacles." In terms of obstacles, the only ground I've found for working with them is practice. Practice is the only thing I've found that really allows me to connect with spaciousness and calm in my mind and from that calm, to see that obstacles are workable and are sometimes not the 'big deal' that our thoughts tell us they are.

For example, one day I was looking out the window in my cell. This was one of the ways I kept my sanity inside. I looked out at a grass courtyard, and saw some rabbits that had burrowed under the fence and were coming in and out of the prison yard. I also saw birds flying in the yard, coming and going freely. Suddenly it occurred to me that neither the birds nor the rabbits had any idea they were in prison. At that moment I also realized that my upset about being in prison was something of a mental construct. So in taking obstacles as a practice, I see them as workable (meaning I don't give up when they get difficult or seem to overwhelm me). I do that through practice and training in holding my mind steady and not getting carried away by my thoughts and emotions. Then I can see that a lot of these thoughts might not be as *real* as I've made them out to be. The next step after that realization is really letting the truth of that penetrate my heart.

I worked as a teacher in prison. I had some of the most wild, dysfunctional, in-your-face type of characters in my classes. And a lot of their acting out and dysfunctionality stemmed from the trouble they had with the process of learning itself. Most had grown up without educational resources in tough areas, and most had not gotten a lot of positive input or encouragement in their childhoods.

The wildest guys seemed to gravitate towards me and want to become my best buddy, a not always comfortable situation. During my time in prison I had many circles of friends. In one of my circle of friends, we'd sometimes make a top ten list of the people who were most irritating, most hated, the biggest assholes in the joint, not something of which I am particularly proud. And then we narrowed it down to the top five to give it more teeth. And we would have funny joking arguments about who was #1. And, wouldn't you know it—I always ended up with all the top five guys from those lists gravitating to me and wanting to be my good buddies. These were the type of guys who would get off a work shift at two in the morning and come back to the cell block, make lots of noise and have no regard for anyone.

The level of inconsiderate behavior in prison is something you just can't fathom. Irritation can come up everywhere and especially when somebody is really in your face. Mostly I would just let the person spin out or I'd walk away. There were a few times when I got back in someone's face—but only a few.

Actually, a week before I left, I had an encounter with someone like that. This guy had been in a word processing class with me and had been kicked out of the class. He was a heavy penitentiary guy, served years and years in prison, he was 6'5", muscle-bound, tattooed, with a deep disdain for anyone who hadn't done hard penitentiary time. I liked the guy, but somehow he got the notion that I was the person who got him kicked out of the class, which was not the case. So, on this day I was walking down a hall and came upon him mopping the floor. In prison, a mop handle is a traditional weapon. I struck up a conversation with him trying to be friendly—and he just went off on me. He was screaming and yelling and threatening me saying if this was a "real pen" he could *really* take care of business! I remained quiet and simply let him blow off steam, I knew that if I got reactionary and back in his face, it would only fuel his fire. He eventually turned away in disgust and I went on my way.

So, what did I learn in prison? I learned that within the context of practice, everything that comes at me in life is workable. I learned that in the face of living among such great suffering and despair, obstacles can become a path and, actually, the fuel for transformation. And for that I am very grateful.

Chapter 9
THE PATH OF SERVICE

I recently presented an Empowerment Model of rehabilitation at a symposium on prison issues at the annual meeting of the American Psychiatric Association. The model is based on a belief in basic human goodness as opposed to the notion of original sin. It builds on a person's strengths rather than focusing on weaknesses. A unique and critical part of this model is *service,* sometimes called socially engaged spirituality. Service provides prisoners with a path or a way to go beyond their own concerns, to make a difference and contribute to other people's lives. The act of service in turn, enriches and transforms their lives in the process. Socially engaged spirituality involves helping others while working on our own spiritual development. In this way, our helping truly benefits those we serve.

We all see suffering in our worlds and want to do something about it. And seeing this suffering or injustice might make us angry. I have a deep connection with prisons, having spent so much time there, so it's easy for me to get angry about the suffering I see there. So how can we relate to the pain and anger that witnessing suffering sometimes inspires?

Many people become social activists out of anger or frustration with systems, which is natural. Perhaps if we didn't feel anger or outrage, we might not be inspired to do anything at all. Thus, anger may motivate us to take positive action to alleviate suffering. But at the same time, this anger may be coming from the inside of us, rather than as a reaction to suffering we see on the outside. It may come from repressed or unacknowledged rage, related to something that happened to us in our past. We might have had experiences that left us with anger and resentment that we are unaware of, and perhaps we've never expressed or even acknowledged this anger to ourselves or anyone else.

So, seeing social injustices or the suffering of others may trigger these repressed feelings and finally provide an outlet for them: "That's horrible, insane, unjust!" We can finally express our anger and frustration, and direct it at something that seems to have little connection to our own pain. If we examine our minds through awareness practices like meditation, then we can possibly see if we are acting out unconscious, personal issues. Because if we are acting our of our own repressed anger—what are we giving to others? What are we sharing? Who are we helping?

There are many volunteers in spiritual communities who do prison work. When a volunteer goes into a prison with resentment towards the system—what are they sharing with prisoners? Are they supporting the prisoner's practice by acting out their unconscious feelings? It's important to stop and look at our intentions if we aspire to address social injustice and reduce suffering. Although, we needn't throw ourselves into such existential doubt that we shrink from the opportunity to help, nevertheless, it's a question of being willing to look at ourselves and our underlying intentions.

In addition to hidden anger, we may also have unmet needs that we bring to the path of service—needs that may include the ways we don't feel supported, nurtured, or loved. Naturally we try to find ways, unconsciously or consciously, to get our needs met. There's nothing wrong with that—the problem is when we're unaware this is what we are doing. I'm not saying that we need to set ridiculously high standards for ourselves—but we could just take a look at ourselves and our intentions.

When we get into helping people there's a natural dualism that arises: "helper" and "helpee," which gets in the way of genuine a genuine connection. Therefore, the socially engaged spirituality, I'm talking about emphasizes a *nondual* approach to service.

What does it mean to operate from a nondual perspective? If we weren't slightly better off or at least think we are in a better situation than those suffering, vulnerable, or disempowered— would we be trying to help? There seems to be an unavoidable dualism here. Is it possible to let go of such identifications and simply be present with the suffering of others, offering our awareness, heart and presence as support without referring back to a strong sense of "I'm doing something here!" or "I'm helping this poor person."

Perhaps the first step is being compassionately aware of these tendencies in ourselves. I did hospice work in prison. It was rewarding and satisfying work in an environment where prisoners are not generally valued or seen as capable of compassion or altruism. I was assigned to at least one patient whom I visited daily, and sometimes two or three patients at a time. When one of my patients got very ill, I'd spend two hours a day—then three, four, five, and—near the end of their lives—most of the day at their bedside, whenever I could get away from my prison job. Sometimes I was able to stay all night when they were close to death. It's quite an undertaking, and occasionally I got very stretched.

Sometimes I was inspired about visiting patients and sometimes not. This was always clear as I walked to the hospital units. I was either inspired or in a neutral space, or I was stressed-out and irritated that I had to go. But I knew that if I didn't go, my patient would feel bad. He expected me to be there for him. The patients counted on us, and often had no one else to look after them. Sometimes things were chaotic, and I didn't have enough time to get my own stuff done. I'd feel like I was spending all of my time taking care of others which sometimes made me resentful, and pissed-off. I'd think, "It's the chaplains fault because they don't recruit enough volunteers," or "The other volunteers are flaky and don't take enough patients and I'm taking this huge load." or "This patient is really demanding—I wish he'd just go away and then I'd only have two patients—blah, blah, blah..." I had thoughts like those. Fortunately, once I saw my patient, all of that usually disappeared and helping him came naturally.

But the interesting part was that walk to the hospital. That's where I really got to look at my mind and motives for doing the work. Where was the resentment coming from? What made me feel claustrophobic, resentful, overworked? What was my connection to this work to begin with? Because if I was doing this not to fulfill my own needs, but to be of service to someone— there wouldn't be a reason for all this discomfort, would there?

That walk to the hospital was an opportunity to see my mind and reflect on my intention. I did an exercise whenever I got to the patient's room. I would stop before going in and clear my mind. It was always interesting to see what was going on right before I stopped. Sometimes seeing how negative my thoughts were would make me feel bad and guilty—but mostly seeing my mind's contortions was kind of liberating. I had the good fortune to see things like that about myself day-in-and day-out. If you do mindfulness and awareness practice, some space comes into your mind, and if you see the same thoughts going through your mind day-in and day-out, it's kind of unavoidable that you'll start to have a sense of humor about it. So there I was walking along, having thoughts like wishing my patient would just get it over with and die, so I that could have more time to write my book about helping people die—and I saw the humor and absurdity of that. I learned that I could have negative thoughts, see them and let them go, and then be present for the person who needed my help.

If we try to solve society's problems without overcoming the confusion and aggression in our own state of mind, our efforts will only contribute to the problem. Isn't the point of spirituality to become a gentle, tamed person who can make a contribution to the world? Or is the point that we should rant and rail at injustice? As a hospice volunteer, when you sit with a person who is laying in bed, emaciated and coughing up phlegm, if you are outraged at the sometimes deplorable conditions people have to die in, or, even if you are terrified yourself of dying—what will you be conveying to this person? Anger and rage about the fact that they're dying in prison and can't go home to their family? Or will you convey presence and kindness—openheartedly being with them in their suffering?

Some people find a conflict between service and practice. The conflict being: do I focus so much on my own spiritual development that I'm shirking my responsibility to others and my world? I might even think, "I'm probably just going to cause more chaos and insanity by trying to help unless I can really develop myself further and get more enlightened," or "The suffering is so pervasive and it has been going on since the beginning of time, so what can I *really* do about it anyway?" Or I could even say "Besides, there's spiritual teachings that say it's all an illusion to begin with— I'd better just focus on my personal practice and try to get enlightened or liberated or sane or something, and not go stir up any more trouble than I already have." So, that's one polarity. The other side is: "The world is going to hell-in-a-handbasket, and if we don't do something about now it it's all going to be over with," or "People who sit around on their butts on a cushion are really just flaking out—there's so much to do." Hopefully, we might find a balance between these two approaches, or somehow transcend this seeming dichotomy altogether.

To be of use to others we need to do two things. The first is to get in touch with our own suffering and pain, to examine whether looking out at the world and seeing the horror and getting outraged might be a way to avoid looking at ourselves. It's easy to look out and see problems—it's harder to look inside and see what's going on. We need to get in touch with our own suffering, pain, anger, frustration, and unmet needs. Chogyam Trungpa taught his students a way to work with this. He called it "Touch and Go." You touch your feelings, allowing yourself to fully experience them, and then you let them go.

The other thing one needs to do to help others, is get in touch with your own basic goodness (*buddhanature*), which means being in touch with your own intrinsic worth and value. We need to connect with the confidence that we have something to give. I'm thoroughly convinced after spending fourteen years in prison with murderers, rapists, bank robbers, child molesters, tax dodgers, drug dealers and every sort of criminal imaginable, that the fundamental nature of all humans beings is good. I have absolutely no doubt in my mind. Not only is our core being essentially good, but we all have tremendous kindness, compassion and natural empathy towards the world and ourselves.

A lot of times it's blocked—it's not that it's *not* there—it's just blocked. So in order to really have something to give to others, as well as getting in touch with our own suffering, we need to get in touch with our own basic goodness. And one of the best ways to achieve both of these things—knowing our pain *and* our goodness—is to practice meditation.

If we are going to help people, we have to learn to be with them, and listen deeply to them before we jump into thinking we have the wisdom necessary to help them with their pain. The natural wisdom that arises from those who are suffering was a great teacher to me. It wasn't necessary for me to be the "Wise Savior." In fact, in many ways, these men were saving me.

I knew a man who got involved with the Buddhist group at the prison, and we became good friends. We had similar backgrounds. He'd been a smuggler too, and he had a son the same age as mine. He never officially became a Buddhist, but he thought of himself as a Buddhist. He'd never gotten involved with a Buddhist community, because he had a fear of getting involved with groups.

I knew he was on the medical floor, but I didn't know why. He was on the floor where people are ambulatory and getting along well. We had a number of videos that dealt with death from a contemplative or Buddhist viewpoint. For the last three months he was there, I noticed he was watching these videos. I began to realize something was wrong. Before he left, he told me he had AIDS. But because he was doing well he was transferred to a general population prison.

At that prison he became very ill, and waited a long time for treatment. Eventually he was sent to an outside hospital and then back to my prison. When he came back I asked if I could be assigned as his hospice volunteer. The chaplain took me up to his room—he was in an isolation room because he had tuberculosis. I was required to wear a surgical mask. I went in, and the chaplain stood outside in the hall. Here was my friend curled up in the bed, emaciated, and really hurting. This was the first time I had seen him in a year and it was really hard for me to see him like that. When he saw me, he sat up and wanted to meditate with me. It was painful for him to sit up, and I tried to get him to lay back down. He told me he'd had a good meditation practice going at the other prison, and there he'd met others who were interested, and they'd started a sitting group that was doing well.

He wanted to sit up and show me that he could still meditate and I kept trying to talk him out of it, trying to get him to lie down and be comfortable. But he insisted and sat up, all skin and bones cross-legged on the bed. I sat on a chair and meditated with him. I was doing okay for a while, but then suddenly I began thinking about TB, and the fact that he and I were sharing the same air and exchanging breaths—since we were sitting very close to each other. I had my mask on, but we were sitting ten inches apart, and the mask had gotten moist with my breath and I knew that once the mask became wet, it was no good. Plus, they can really only offer protection for ten minutes and we'd been sitting fifteen—and then twenty. We were nose to nose— and I started to panic.

I'd been doing hospice work for a long time. I've also been a Buddhist for a long time, studied the *Tibetan Book of the Dead* teachings, taught meditation classes and trained hospice volunteers. I thought I'd processed most of my fear around death, and thought I had a handle on it. But in this situation the panic built and built and built. And pretty soon I just couldn't take it—I had to get out of the room.

Actually the chaplain told me I couldn't stay long, because I wasn't assigned as my friend's hospice volunteer yet, and there wasn't clearance to go into his room since he was in strict isolation. The chaplain had only allowed us to visit for fifteen minutes. It had been twenty-five minutes, and the chaplain hadn't knocked on the door. I was thinking "*Where* is he?—Please knock on the door and get me out of here!" But he never knocked, and finally, I couldn't take the panic. so I left. I then realized I had a way to go working with the fear of death.

Service can push our buttons, it can bring up our own stuff, and illuminate where we are stuck, and where we have fears or resistance. If you can see those 'hot spots'—acknowledge them, and then let them go—that's one way of not getting stuck. Because we don't really get stuck in *their* stuff and *their* problems—we get stuck in our own. I learned a lot about where I was stuck in my years of hospice work. I also got a great lesson in seeing the problems I had working with people in pain. I am forever grateful to those great teachers—the dying men I worked with, man of whom became dear friends.

Getting out of myself and serving others is a powerful tool that, in my experience, was the main key to my transformation in prison. I believe that the world might change for the better if enough of us shifted our focus toward helping others who need us. I truly hope that more and more prisoners will find opportunities for service in their world. Service doesn't have to be a big deal or project, it can come in all shapes and forms: hospice work, starting meditation groups, or even just simple kindness or learning how to deeply listen to another's pain. Wouldn't it be great to transform America's prisons so that they become a source—not for crime and violence—but for positive social change?